Musings from a Pandemic
PETER BARBER'S MUSINGS
BOOK TWO

PETER BARBER

ILLUSTRATED BY
CHARLY ALEX FULLER

Ant Press
Large Print
Edition

Please note that this book is the original creation of the author. The author wrote and compiled it entirely without the use of any artificial intelligence.

USE OF THIS BOOK FOR AI TRAINING:

Without in any way limiting the author's and publisher's exclusive rights under copyright, any use of this publication to "train" generative artificial intelligence (AI) technologies to generate text is expressly prohibited. The author reserves all rights to license uses of this work for generative AI training and development of machine learning language models.

Copyright © 2024 Peter Barber

Formatted and published by Ant Press, 2024

Cover and interior illustrations by Charly Alex Fuller

ISBN: 9781916574199 Paperback

ISBN: 9781916574205 Hardback

ISBN: 9781916574212 Large Print Paperback

ISBN: 9781916574229 Large Print Hardback

All rights reserved.

No part of this book may be reproduced in any form or by any electronic or mechanical means, including information storage and retrieval systems, without written permission from the author, except for the use of brief quotations in a book review.

Contents

Over to Anne	xi
Preface	xv

Day 1 — 1
House arrest

Day 2 — 5
This is going to be really boring

Day 3 — 8
Sneeze and share

Day 4 — 11
Shaken, not stirred

Day 5 — 14
Isn't technology wonderful?

Day 6 — 17
Today I was so bored I decided to chew my foot off

Day 7 — 20
Latest News

Day 8 — 23
Even my car wants to stay at home

Day 9 — 27
My boot is now open!

Day 10 — 31
Bats and Corona beer

Day 11 *Big Brother is watching*	35
Day 12 *Covid-19 protection cocktail bath*	40
Day 13 *Brexit*	45
Day 14 *5G Wi-Fi system will spread the virus*	49
Day 15 *Stay off my sticky tape!*	54
Day 16 *Jehovah's Witnesses were right all along*	58
Day 17 *Heineken. Refreshes the parts other beers cannot reach*	62
Day 18 *A different way of greeting*	67
Day 19 *Boost your immune system*	71
Day 20 *You never know who's watching*	75
Day 21 *Please, Boris*	80
Day 22 *Breaking news*	84
Day 23 *Motorway Grand Prix*	90

Day 24   95
Daily walk for sale

Day 25   99
A little more serious today

Day 26   102
The tests are falling far short

Day 27   107
Postcard from my holiday

Day 28   112
Turkish Delight

Day 29   116
Now one for the children

Day 30   122
Alternative medicine

Day 31   126
Letter to America

Day 32   131
Dear Mr Secret Service

Day 33   136
Interview with a virus

Day 34   141
I think I was patient zero

Day 35   146
Recipes for pigeon

Day 36   151
My wife is becoming a bit twitchy

Day 37 *The following information could save your life*	155
Day 38 *Don't read the ingredients*	160
Day 39 *How dare they let me in!*	165
Day 40 *I like it with extra hair and nipples*	169
Day 41 *I thought I would start with cooking something small*	173
Day 42 *A funny thing about bananas*	177
Day 43 *A frown creeps across my face as my brain cells kick in*	181
Day 44 *I now have bigger boobs than my wife*	185
Day 45 *Hay fever season is here*	189
Day 46 *My little dog is a bit different*	194
Day 47 *Sorry? Run that past me again ...*	199
Day 48 *Not only is it really hard to watch ...*	202
Day 49 *My wife has a thing about washing stuff*	206

Day 50	211
I told you I was ill	
Day 51	216
A war on fat people	
Day 52	219
It's the Eurovision Song Contest time	
Day 53	224
I'm fat	
Day 54	228
Trust yourselves	
Day 55	233
Back to work	
Day 56	237
Freedom at last	
About the Author	241
Contacts and Links	243
More Ant Press Books	246

With immense joy, I dedicate this book to Anne Cooper. Anne encouraged and propelled me forward on my writing journey. Her kind words and daily messages of fun and laughter spurred me on as a new writer. If I could make one person laugh, why not everybody? When she told me that my writing helped ease her suffering during her long battle with Covid, it was all the encouragement I needed.
Because of Anne's kind words, I realised I'd made a difference in one person's life. I went on to write my popular Parthenon series about life in Greece. Every time I started a new book, I heard Anne's voice in my mind saying, "Do it, Peter! Do it!"
Thank you, Anne. I did it for you.

Over to Anne

I first "met" Peter in 2020 on Facebook. At that time I was off work, suffering from what was to be my first bout of Covid. He posted daily "Texts from Dad" telling of how he was adapting to the new normal. I was hooked; I could empathise! He told of his trips out, the "six-foot rule" and, of course, his shopping, which always included beer.

One day, I got in touch with him via email and told him how much I enjoyed his posts, and to my surprise, he very kindly sent me two signed copies. When I was unable to sleep at night, out came my "Covid bible" and I would read for hours.

One morning my kids, Leanne and James, asked, "Could we hear you laughing last night?" This was something they hadn't heard for some time. I had turned a small corner. We were in quarantine, and going out was a risk, but every day I joined Peter on his walks with his dogs and joined in Alexandra's Zumba class. I was living vicariously through Peter's writing, and I wanted to read more.

Peter said that he was writing about his life in Greece with Alexandra, and he was thinking of publishing it. Do it, Peter! Do it! Here I was, a dumpy little lass waving her pompoms and cheering him on from the sidelines! Book after book came out and I realised that I wasn't the only one who

OVER TO ANNE

could spot a brilliant book when they read one.

Well, Peter, from posting on Facebook to publications in the Number One spot worldwide — you've smashed it, ducky! Keep on writing and making so many people happy. It's such an honour to have a book dedicated to me. I'm nobody, just a mum of two who loves to read. I am SO happy and blessed to call you friends.

PS: Please don't miss out "You can tell all that from one finger?"! Cracks me up every time.

Preface

Most of us had never experienced a lockdown. It was a strange and worrying time for us all. We did not know how bad the virus was going to be. People were dying, others were becoming sick, and information was garbled and confusing.

Alex and I live between England and Greece. We left Greece and planned to stay in our home in Dunstable, England, when the potential of coronavirus became apparent. We would watch the news updates and see the global drama unfolding as we considered if we should remain in the UK or fly back to Greece. But the choice was made when the British government decided for us.

Most of us saw the lockdown coming. Italy

PREFACE

had been in lockdown for a while after being the first to suffer the ravages of this new, unknown affliction. The only real surprise was that the British government waited so long.

On 23 March 2020, they ordered us to stay at home.

My daughter lives close by in a small house with her husband, four children and a dog. Like everybody, she was worried. After all, it was all anyone could think of at the time.

So, I decided to launch a little project to keep her busy. I would write a daily post, email it to her, and she would post it on her Facebook page. I just wanted to make her laugh. If she could get involved in my pet project, then perhaps I could encourage her to smile and busy herself with something other than facing future uncertainty.

As we got further into our imprisonment, it was becoming increasingly clear that the lunatics were running the asylum. Conflicting advice was being thrown at us daily, adding to the confusion felt by us all.

I didn't want to make these posts too serious. I wanted to use humour to help us cope with our imposed robotic existence. So, I decided on a different approach and formed them into a daily diary describing what we were all

PREFACE

going through at the time, but from a different perspective.

Instead of joining the millions of frightened people, adding to their concerns, I would make them laugh instead.

Humour has developed over thousands of years as humans have evolved. It is a coping mechanism which helps us to weather the storms of tragedy. It can lift us from sadness, and give us a way of refreshing ourselves, helping us to face the world again. Sometimes, laughter can be a manic defence, like a coping strategy but in a protective way. It will divert the reality of what's happening and the reality of loss and human vulnerability. This is why some people laugh during funeral services. Laughter and sadness are two sides of the same coin. We need them both.

I would often receive a call from my daughter. "Dad, you can't write that," she'd say, followed by a giggle.

But I did anyway.

As she began her daily posts, she gained a significant following. After the first week, they were being shared and growing in popularity. With nothing else to occupy them, people were spending more time on social media. Towards the end of the lockdown, she was receiving

PREFACE

hundreds of likes every day. Together, we were getting people to laugh again.

But unknown to me, she had kept all my posts, added her illustrations, and sent them to a publisher who decided to form them into a book and launch to the world. Our book was born.

Humour has always been the best medicine, so read on and remember. I do hope it brings a smile.

Day 1
HOUSE ARREST

24th March 2020

I'm trapped! A prisoner. House arrest. Confined to barracks. Only allowed to drive to supermarkets, nowhere else. Only allowed to walk once a day, but don't drive there – stay close to home.

Yesterday Boris Johnson made his televised announcement that Great Britain is now closed. After weeks of dithering, he has finally announced the following new rules:

1. Stay at home.
2. Go shopping only for basic necessities.
3. One form of exercise a day – either alone or with members of your household.
4. Leave home only for medical needs or to provide care or help vulnerable persons.
5. Travel to work – but only if necessary, and you cannot work from home.

This has been coming for a couple of weeks. Last week he announced that although the pubs can remain open, nobody should go there. Restaurants and theatres should be avoided at all costs, but are still allowed to remain open.

Prior to this, the main government advice

was to wash your hands while singing "Happy Birthday" twice.

Now everything must close. No more football, no more TV sport, no more wandering aimlessly around the shops to buy tat that you don't need. What will we do with our time? By the way, what are basic necessities? I hope it includes beer.

Schools started to close on 18 March. Restaurants were forced to close on 20 March, and my favourite pub closed its doors on Friday 20 March at seven minutes past eight. I distinctly remember the time because my watch broke while I was being dragged by my feet away from the bar, leaving furrows on the wood from my fingernails while trying to cling on for a few more minutes, begging for just one more beer.

So, I can't go to work. I'm disappointed that I can't go to the gym. I did join over a year ago on a sudden impulse to get in shape, but I never went. I would have liked to start now, but that's closed, too. I can always assure my wife that I was going to get in shape, but the government wouldn't let me. That may work.

As I'll have to stay at home, I will need to plan this very carefully. Soon Alex will realise that I am sitting around doing nothing and start getting ideas of how to keep me occupied. This is likely to include gardening and home improvements. I already have the excuse that no hardware shops will be open so will probably get away with decorating. Getting out of digging the garden will be a little more challenging, but it might rain, I hope.

Boris has promised an update on the lockdown in three weeks. This will certainly be extended. I think we are likely to be trapped for at least two months, so we need to start getting used to it. Quietly looking forward to doing nothing for a while anyhow.

Day 2
THIS IS GOING TO BE REALLY BORING

25th March 2020

Currently not working so decided to send daily posts to my daughter. Strange how human behaviour has changed in a week. We thought ventilators were things to keep you cool on a warm day. Dyson has been asked to make some ventilators in his vacuum cleaner factory. I hope he remembers to ensure that it blows not sucks.

Shaking hands is right out, kissing banned. Violence will now be confined to verbal abuse as no touching allowed.

In the old days you used to cough to cover a fart. Now we have to fart to cover a cough as coughing is really embarrassing. Safe sex used to be wearing a condom. Now it involves a spacesuit, large quantities of viral handwash and staying two metres apart.

Tube train timetable has been cut in half, ensuring passengers that need to work have to stand close together. Brilliant solution. Hospitals only testing patients that already have the virus. Not doctors or nurses who are more likely to get it.

Government promises something they are calling the furlough scheme. They will be paying us 80 per cent of our wages to stay at home. Wow. This seems a suspiciously good deal. There are bound to be a lot of strings attached to this idea. Not seen it yet. Perhaps they are trying to thin the herd first. There is talk of herd immunity being favoured by Boris. That didn't work very well with bubonic plague, but perhaps he hasn't read the history books. Or perhaps he has, and it's a cunning plan to ensure nobody receives the dosh.

Day 3
SNEEZE AND SHARE

26th March 2020

Has anyone noticed how difficult it is to suppress a sneeze? I went shopping for essentials (mostly beer). Nearly my turn at the checkout keeping the regulation two metres apart. Needed to sneeze and must have had a blowback as my eyes bulged and I went deaf. I think I got away with it and don't think anyone noticed. Better now, though.

As I am now working mostly from home, I was asked to join a FaceTime conference. For someone that's never even taken a selfie this was a new experience for me. Turned my phone camera on, couldn't see anything as every time I pointed the camera to my face all I could see was the back of the phone. Then found the button to rotate the picture. Staring back at me was this old-looking wreck, saggy bags under the eyes and unruly grey hair. It was me! As the only time I look in the mirror is when I shave, the reflection is usually misty and my face covered in shaving foam, so I don't really take too much notice. Now I saw this strange-looking old guy who was copying every expression.

Self-image is an interesting thing. Until that point, I was sure that I was average-looking and fairly presentable. I think my phone camera may be faulty so will go off for a new one. Maybe that will work better.

This morning, I had to drive into London on government-sanctioned essential business. First time ever there was no traffic and empty roads. Extinction Rebellion must think all their birthdays have come at once. Few cars, fewer lorries and no aeroplanes circling in the sky. I parked outside the site on an empty road, not a soul in sight.

Suddenly, a voice behind me said, "You can't park there."

It was a traffic warden.

Some things never change.

Day 4

SHAKEN, NOT STIRRED

27th March 2020

I suspect that I know where all the hand sanitiser has gone. With pubs closed and wine bars a thing of the past, people have realised it's almost pure alcohol so are using it with ice and tonic, with little umbrellas. When this is all over, we will have developed a taste for it and be using it as a new cocktail ingredient.

We must now have the cleanest hands in the history of the human race. The government has told us not to touch our faces. We have never been embarrassed to scratch our nose before. In the old days you had to adopt ingenious ways to scratch your bum in public, like altering the way you walk in an attempt to rub your bottom cheeks to add pressure to the itch. Now we have to consider a similar strategy if our nose itches. It is no longer acceptable to put our hand anywhere near our face and will now cause more embarrassment in public than scratching our bottom.

In the future, parents will be able to prove that biting your nails can be hazardous, thumb-sucking extremely dangerous, and picking your nose could kill you. Touching other bits is okay, for now, but you might still go blind.

OTHER NEWS

Boris Johnson has reported that he has coronavirus. I hope he hasn't been kissing Dominic Cummings. That would be a shame.

Day 5
ISN'T TECHNOLOGY WONDERFUL?

28th March 2020

MUSINGS FROM A PANDEMIC

Just received a text that said *Skype me*. *What???* Is this a new pick-up line or a direct offer that passed me by? Is someone flirting with me? Obviously they haven't seen my selfie. In the old days, flirting required chocolates and flowers, but now the direct approach seems quite fashionable, I think.

After a little research, I found out what Skype is. Bit disappointing. Isn't technology wonderful? Well, it might be if I could understand any of it, coming from a generation that only had telephones connected to the wall by a wire, and Betamax video recorders that only a genius could program. My first computer was a ZX Spectrum that needed an audiocassette tape to load it. It took me weeks to realise that it had to be a special audio cassette as anything from the Rolling Stones upset it. The first-ever internet was through a modem that made strange noises while taking twenty minutes to load.

Now, in the days of self-isolation we are encouraged to have virtual meetings. This seems to involve talking to someone on the TV. I have personally been shouting at the TV for years, but the bloody thing has never answered me back before. What would my grandmother have made of this?

PETER BARBER

❊ ❊ ❊

Just came back from the supermarket. Needed more essentials (mostly beer). The new system is to form an orderly queue outside, two metres apart, and then be let in one at a time. Standing in the queue for thirty minutes with freezing wind and rain lashing sideways, I think I caught pneumonia. So the new system designed to stop you getting pneumonia can give you a different pneumonia. Makes sense.

Day 6

TODAY I WAS SO BORED I DECIDED TO CHEW MY FOOT OFF

29th March 2020

To my horror I found that I couldn't reach my foot. I didn't realise I was so unfit and overweight. I know my foot is still there, although I haven't seen it for a while due to the thicker jumpers I've been wearing recently, and also because my six-pack seems to have transformed into a party barrel. So I decided to take my equally unfit and overweight dogs for an extended drag across the fields in an attempt to get fit again, or more accurately, for the first time since puberty.

People do have to realise that you cannot get coronavirus from saying "Good morning". As I approached another chap leading his dog over the field, I noticed him change his direction to arc around me, giving me about five metres' clearance while not looking directly at me.

"Good morning," I yelled.

He didn't reply and just pulled his hat further over his face and looked away. The next dog owner did exactly the same. A chap on a bike rode slowly towards me. This time, before he started his arc I yelled, "Good morning." A panicky look spread over his face. His bike wobbled before recovering and speeding away from me without any reply. This is called social distancing.

On returning from my walk I checked my feet. No. Still can't see them, so same again tomorrow.

MUSINGS FROM A PANDEMIC

So. What are we going to do with all the cardboard centres of the millions of toilet rolls that have been panic-bought? When I was a kid we used to watch *Blue Peter* which would show you how to make stuff. We could try sellotaping them together as tubes for the new Dyson ventilators. Link up two with string, and we will still have communication after the telephones get cut off. Or use them as telescopes to spy on your neighbour. I'm sure the old lady up the road went for two walks yesterday.

I hear that the Mercedes F1 team are starting to make ventilators. These will need to be retuned otherwise the poor patients will be hyperventilating, but the NHS should get them really quickly. When the rest of the F1 teams catch on, we can watch live coverage of the race to deliver their stuff to the hospitals. This should be done in an organised manner with commentary by Murray Walker, pit stops for tyres, and a chequered flag at the end to see who won.

Day 7
LATEST NEWS

30th March 2020

MUSINGS FROM A PANDEMIC

Dominic Cummings, the prime minister's chief adviser, has been reported to have symptoms of coronavirus. More good news. The Downing Street cat is fine.

Alex, being a Zumba enthusiast, has been like a caged lion at home since her twenty-six weekly Zumba sessions were cancelled. But she has now discovered that she can still take part in her favourite activity in front of her laptop in the living room. This is all fine, but I spend my time having my ears assaulted by Latino music while huddling in the corner trying to avoid being kicked to death. I did suggest that she took up a safer hobby like bomb disposal. At least it would be quieter (most of the time).

I heard today that a new symptom of coronavirus is loss of taste and smell. I personally have never had taste. I once painted all my walls brown to match my orange PVC furniture. Luckily, I have a rather windy Labrador who keeps reminding me that I haven't got coronavirus.

PETER BARBER

Just been to the supermarket for some essentials (mostly beer). As I have been making my own bread recently, I was looking for some yeast. All sold out. If anyone knows where I can get some, please let me know. Please avoid the Canesten cream, though, as it upsets the yeast and makes the bread taste funny.

Day 8

EVEN MY CAR WANTS TO STAY AT HOME

31st March 2020

Our family cars have realised that the entire country is now in lockdown, so, not wishing to be left out, they've decided to join in and relax a little too.

Been outside hitting my car with a hammer. We were going to visit my aged father-in-law, who is self-isolating, to deliver supplies. Loaded all the shopping into Alex's car. Went to start it but battery flat. So transferred all shopping into the boot of my car. Closed the boot lid. Went to start the car. Dashboard bleeped to inform me that the boot was open. Went back to the boot but it was closed. Pressed the button to open it again. It was stuck.

What happened to the cars of the old days? Those were easy. If it didn't start, you could get someone to give it a push. There was no such thing as central locking, or automatic boot lids.

No cars should have computers – if they go wrong, nothing works.

After two hours of swearing at it while trying everything to lever it up, I gave up. Not too bothered about the boot; I was more concerned that it was stuffed with shopping bags. Also worried about another trip to the supermarket to replace everything. I'm sure that security guard in Tesco's will recognise me.

Perhaps I can borrow Alex's mask and go in disguise. But after a few days I think the shopping in my car will start to decay, and I'm a bit worried about the fresh fish in the shopping bags. Luckily the windows still open so I should be able to keep the smell at bay for a while.

I decided to jumpstart Alex's car. But the booster cables are in the bloody boot that won't open. Called automobile association who came out and started the car but informed me it would not start again as the battery had died and needed urgent replacement. Went to get a new battery fitted. Queued up at the supermarket for an hour to replace the shopping that is currently stuck in the boot of the other car. Came home. Gave keys and shopping to Alex to take to aged father-in-law while I went for a lie-down.

Anyway. Now all the gymnasiums are closed, and we are all limited to one walk a day. Found a good way to legally exercise and sneak another walk. You can go to the supermarket. Push twenty linked trolleys around the car park for an hour and it only costs £1. And the best part is, you can get the £1 back.

Day 9

MY BOOT IS NOW OPEN!

1st April 2020

After locking my shopping in the car yesterday and spending most of the day trying to lever the boot open, I have good news. My boot is now open! I went out to the car this morning with a selection of power tools, ready to brutalise my shiny Jaguar. Plugged in the drill, put my welding mask on. I thought I would press the boot release just one more time. It opened.

It's been a stubborn car since I got it. It tends to default to restricted performance when it's tired just to slow me down a bit, and it frequently shows me warning lights on the dash just to frighten me. A couple of days ago, a red error message flashed up while I was driving at 70 mph on the motorway, indicating that I had a flat rear tyre, so stop immediately. False alarm again.

So the sight of me approaching with a power drill and welding equipment must have scared it because it could see I was serious this time.

❊ ❊ ❊

President Trump has announced that people should wear scarves if they can't find masks. The only one I have is a Watford football scarf.

However, as I live dangerously close to Luton, I am likely to get attacked by the locals. But it would only be a verbal assault as they have to stay two metres away.

※ ※ ※

Like most people staying at home, I wake up in the morning and go through the coronavirus checklist. Am I coughing? No. How's my temperature? Fine. Can I still taste my breakfast? Check. Can I still smell my windy Labrador? Check. So, all fine for today at least. But now that winter flu has started to go away, hay fever season will soon be on us. Symptoms include sneezing and coughing, a runny or blocked nose, loss of smell, pain around your temples and forehead, and a headache.

On average, one in five people get hay fever in this country. Initial symptoms are very similar to coronavirus. This means there will likely be an additional 14 million people self-isolating because they will definitely assume that they have Covid-19. This is in addition to the people that have got the virus or other assorted allergies. At least the supermarkets will be less busy. Perhaps the government should directly employ all people suffering from hay fever and place them strategically outside places the government don't want us to go. One sight of somebody sneezing and snuffling in the street will certainly deter most people.

It's a common mistake people make that diarrhoea is a symptom of coronavirus. This is not true. It is caused by the fear of coronavirus. This is the real reason supermarket shoppers are standing two metres apart.

Day 10

BATS AND CORONA BEER

2nd April 2020

It's not as bad as it looks.

One good thing to come out of the current pandemic is that we have put aside racism and homophobia in favour of protecting our own skins. Brexit has been forgotten. Nobody cares about the colour or creed of people any more, whether gay or straight, black, white or brown. None of this matters, as long as their first name is doctor or nurse.

However, us humans, being generally bigoted and simple pack animals – some even get past Page Three of *The Sun* and read the words (only the little ones, though) – still need something to hate. So let's all forget previous prejudice and gang up on the bats. After all, they are the little bastards that gave us this virus in the first place.

Okay. Strictly speaking, we shouldn't be eating them, but the point still stands. There they are, hanging around in their caves looking furry and cute, completely ignoring the rules on social distancing. Going out more than once a day to bite necks. All packed upside down in little rows, infecting each other before flapping their way to the nearest Chinese food market to give us the bug.

We could start by infecting them with a huge dose of human racism; we have plenty of that to spare. This would then turn the fruit bats against the vampires. And the pipistrelles against the long-eared brown ones. Soon, entire species of bats would be so preoccupied with trying to wipe each other out that they wouldn't get time to be eaten. Problem solved.

The only problem I can see with this is how to get close enough to infect them. The little buggers have radar, so they will know you're coming.

While visiting my supermarket to buy some essentials (mostly beer), I noted there were still empty shelves where the toilet rolls used to be and to my horror, the beer shelves seemed empty! The only beer available was Corona, and it was on special offer. Are people really that stupid? Do people actually think they can get coronavirus from a beer with the same first name? Obviously, the answer is a resounding "Yes".

The people that avoid Corona beer still look fairly normal from the outside. They still walk (but usually drag their knuckles) and breathe (mostly out of their mouths). They hold down jobs, vote (usually for Brexit), and have opinions (mostly those given to them from *The Sun* newspaper though). They are likely to hoard toilet rolls although they have no idea what to do with them. They save money on masks by wearing them one day and turning them around the next, and have seven or eight kids but have no idea where babies come from.

So, I got some Corona beer. Going to boil it first, though, just to be safe.

Day 11

BIG BROTHER IS WATCHING

3rd April 2020

The government has decided to bring forward the release of criminals due to coronavirus in prisons. They still have to self-isolate like the rest of us, but don't get three meals a day cooked for them and will have to make their own beds. They are allowed to keep their masks, but will need to sew up the eyeholes and adapt the stockings. I think that the government feels safe as most of the banks are closed, but are using the army to guard the toilet rolls. Some convicts currently finishing their shifts on escape-tunnel digging have emerged to find that everyone has gone home and turned the lights off.

The police have been given sweeping new powers to stop, question and fine people who break the curfew. The government are rubbing their sanitised hands together at the prospect of keeping these newly acquired laws after the current pandemic is over. These convenient new powers are like the Big Bad Wolf following the Three Little Piggies home, but only to protect them.

Trying to wrestle these new powers back from the police will be like trying to take a bone from a feral dog, only with more blood involved. In the future we will still be told when we are permitted to go to the supermarket, how many walks we are allowed per day, how long we can spend in the toilet ...

The Chinese are using an app that tracks every movement and every contact you make. The divorce rate will skyrocket. The app will show exactly which pub you have attended, when, and who with. No more pretending to go to the supermarket and dropping in for a quick half at your local. Betting shops will close permanently, and brothels will insist you leave your phone at the church around the corner.

Google will be delighted at the increase in advertising revenue. They can track you in real-time and flog stuff to you based on your exact location, immediately pinging it to your phone.

- Too much time standing up in the toilet: adverts for prostate checks.
- Too much time sitting on the toilet: adverts for toilet paper and magazines.
- Too much time at the pick and mix counter in Asda: adverts for toothpaste and dentists.
- Too much time at the church: adverts for condoms.

The list goes on.

The only way to avoid this will be to leave your phone at home. There will be lost people wandering aimlessly around the streets with no access to Google Maps, not knowing what to buy at the shops because they had texted the shopping list to themselves and forgotten how to use a pencil. The new coronavirus hospitals will be repurposed to treat phone withdrawal symptoms and the NHS will be overwhelmed again.

※ ※ ※

Just returned from my daily one walk allowed. I downloaded this new app on my phone that is called MapMyRun. This app will tell me the distance I have run (in my case wandered at a slow pace): speed, pace, stride length, and a full GPS map of my route travelled. Understanding technology not being my strong point, so far I have only worked out which button starts it. Not sure about how to stop it yet.

So, walking boots on, dogs on leads, off we go.

After 15 minutes I took my phone out of my pocket.

Read the screen. Time elapsed: 14 minutes. Distance: 0.

A further 10 minutes elapsed. Time elapsed: 25 minutes. Distance: 0.

Got home, looked again. Time elapsed: 45 minutes. Distance: 0.

Pressed a few more random buttons and found out that I was apparently on treadmill mode. So this all-dancing, highly technological new app has no idea that it's been anywhere. As my phone has now told me that I haven't left home today, does that mean that I can still get my one walk a day? Again?

I might go out for a walk later.

Day 12

COVID-19 PROTECTION COCKTAIL BATH

4th April 2020

In these days of staying at home and self-isolating, our lives seem to have changed in unexpected ways. As all televised sport has been cancelled, HDTV has really gone downhill. Most of what we see is from webcams showing various politicians, specialists and presenters peering at you through their grainy laptop camera which keeps freezing. So we're forced to take our eyes off the TV screen and look around. Who is this person sitting next to me on the sofa? She seems very nice but I haven't really noticed her before. Oh yes, I remember, I married her in 1975.

Our eyes are reopening to our environment. Noticing the little bit of flaking paintwork on the stairs, the recess in the sofa that has been created by long years of slouching watching sport, the worn-out patch of veneer on the coffee table where my beer used to be placed. Realising that I have trouble seeing because my hair is too long and I'm not allowed to get a haircut. Glancing at the calendar on the wall, which reminds me that my birthday was a couple of months ago, but as I was too busy watching another rerun of the 1966 World Cup final, I completely missed it.

Watching the clock tick on to nowhere special as nothing is planned. Great, isn't it?

Looking forward to doing the same again tomorrow.

PETER BARBER

❋ ❋ ❋

Due to government advice we have to take one walk a day. Being a law-abiding citizen, I am following their rules. This is all new to me. In the old days, walking was confined to as little as possible. This was usually to get from my house to the car, and then from the supermarket car park for a quick wander around the store to buy mostly beer, then back to the car. That was my exercise regime.

Now we have to actually leave home and go somewhere, and we're not allowed to take the car to get there. Wandering across the local fields, past the ancient remnants of the football pitch with its slowly decaying goalposts, the empty playground with half a seesaw, a brown patch on the ground where the old burnt-out stolen car used to be …

In the future, climate change activists will have had their way and we will all be living in caves and eating foxes. Future generations will look at these old remnants of civilisation and ask their grandfathers what this ancient game of football was all about. Not looking forward to that though, as they would have to try explaining the offside rule again.

MUSINGS FROM A PANDEMIC

Hand sanitiser is still not available in shops. Alex had the bright idea of using nail varnish remover instead. She assured me that as it is mostly alcohol, it must do the same job. Didn't work out very well, though. I scratched my eye and my contact lens melted, and I constantly smell like pear drops.

Frequent washing and the use of hand sanitisers have really taken their toll. Mine have gone all wrinkly. I would expect this to be the new way of life and future generations will start to develop webbed fingers.

My wife has really taken this seriously as whenever I return from my compulsory daily walk or buying essential supplies from the supermarket (mostly beer), I return home to find her dressed in her home-made nuclear protection suit, directing me through the sheep-dip pit in the garden filled with foot-and-mouth prevention wash, then into the pre-prepared Covid-19 protection cocktail bath of Domestos and Dettol. Can't lounge around too long in the bath because of the danger of melting. Getting suspicious, though, as we just saw the movie about John Haigh, the Acid

PETER BARBER

Bath Murderer, on Netflix, so she might be getting ideas of adding a little sulphuric acid to the cocktail. Not too worried about my hands, it's the rest of me that needs ironing.

Day 13
BREXIT

5th April 2020

I remember the Brexit bus proudly announcing that we can give an additional 350 million per week to the NHS, while the government has embarked on an austerity programme to cut 360 million per week through the back door.

Now the entire country is on lockdown. Brexit has been put aside while we look to protecting our own arses. But rest assured, the subject is far from forgotten in the dark, dingy basement of Downing Street. Right now, new slogans are being prepared to replace the other profound three-word sentences:

"Take Back Control".

"Brexit Means Brexit".

And my all-time favourite: "Get It Done".

This will then be launched onto the masses through the pipeline of their tame right-wing media and favourite websites. They will assure us that it will be much better to self-isolate the United Kingdom from the bureaucratic European Union, who are determined to straighten out our bananas and ban smoky bacon crisps.

Now the inconvenient Germans have thrown a spanner in the works by accepting and testing coronavirus samples from NHS staff because they can get the results quicker and more efficiently. As over 20 per cent of NHS workers in this country are non-British and mostly EU nationals, we can rest assured that these embarrassing facts will not go on the side of the next bus. Unfortunately, the company that made the last bus went into liquidation because of the slowdown of the economy due to Brexit. The government will have to buy the next one from Germany and pay the tariffs to import it.

Boris Johnson won over the northern unemployed miners during the last election campaign by promising blue passports and more fish. They forgot that the Conservative Party under Maggie Thatcher wiped out all mining jobs, together with the rest of British industry, in favour of the banking sector. Look at how that worked out.

You ask the average man in the street why he voted for Brexit. The reply is usually related to trade: import and export, and their concern about the current balance of payment account. Nothing to do with the Polish plumber that they perceive to have taken their job and their hospital appointment.

These people wouldn't know a trade deficit report if it hit them between the eyes. Most need to take their shoes off to count to eleven. But when you point out that import and export is going to be a real problem with lorries stacked from Dover to Watford Gap at two metres apart, they will usually quote information that's been spoon-fed to them by the *Daily Telegraph* telling them that we can trade on World Trade Organisation rules.

They have no idea the World Trade Organisation consists of a small office above a shop in Düsseldorf with one member of staff who only comes in once a day to feed the cat. The good news is that we might have left the biggest economic market in the world but may be able to negotiate free-trade agreements with other economic giants like Zimbabwe or the Cook Islands. We might even be able to secure a tariff-free deal with China. Not too keen on the last thing they exported to us tariff-free, though.

But we live in a democracy, so we must allow these people to vote. Lucky for them the election system in this country only requires you to spell X, so I think we are all doomed.

This is likely to piss off the 51.9 per cent of people that voted for Brexit. But I am relying on the fact that I have used long sentences and largely avoided three-word slogans, so hopefully they might miss it.

In these difficult times, we are all in it together, so let's stick together and get through it.

Don't worry. Had my rant, so back to normal tomorrow.

Day 14

5G WI-FI SYSTEM WILL SPREAD THE VIRUS

6th April 2020

Did you know that you can get coronavirus by text? No, nor did I. Apparently there are some people out there that score a minus on an IQ test.

These strange individuals have seen somewhere that the new 5G Wi-Fi system will spread the virus. This is based on the assumption that Wuhan in China has lots of these masts, and they know for a fact that these are responsible for the current worldwide pandemic. So, they have taken it into their small brains to make it their mission to destroy all 5G communication in this country.

They haven't realised yet that there are more of these masts in Beijing than Wuhan, and almost nobody has it there. Japan hasn't even got one of these 5G masts and has still declared a state of emergency. Some of the countries suffering from this nasty disease haven't even got electricity, never mind Wi-Fi.

Undeterred, these mind-numbingly stupid people have decided to burn all cell phone towers in their region. These deluded individuals with no capacity for any sort of logical thought are actually spending their time climbing these towers, armed with an oily rag and a gallon of petrol, to protect us. The only real mystery is how they recognise 5G equipment in the first place. To date we have lost around 15 of the new 5G towers, 250 electrical pylons and another 900 lamp posts. One of the more successful morons managed to scale the tower and fall off, breaking his leg in two places, but couldn't call for help as his mobile phone didn't work.

But they mean well.

※ ※ ※

My Zumba-fanatic wife has been having severe withdrawal symptoms because her eight daily sessions have been cancelled. She has tried virtual Zumba on the laptop but claims it's not the same. So she has decided to use her one walk a day to take our two unfit and overweight dogs for a jog across the nearby farmland. These dogs are used to a quick wander in the local small park to do a little business and have a sniff at a few lamp posts, while keeping up to date on their doggie pals that live in the area.

All in all, the daily walk is usually over in about fifteen minutes before returning for a nice bowl of Pedigree Chum and a six-hour sleep to recover. Now they are expected to run across the nearby farmland, trying to keep up at a pace that would scare a long-distance marathon athlete. And instead of a quick wander around the park, it's a full three-mile run.

Well, this was her plan.

After the first half mile, she noticed that the dogs were no longer following. Looking back, she saw them both sitting on the footpath, tongues hanging out, refusing to go any further. When she returned home, the dogs collapsed in the garden and refused to move, even when tempted by their favourite snack of pigs' ears.

So today she tried again.

Normally the dogs will see the leads and realise the walk is coming. They'll bounce excitedly around the house, delighted that they are going out. Today, leads ready, no response. Went to find them. One was trembling in the kitchen, the other upstairs hiding in the wardrobe. No jogging for them today, then.

❖ ❖ ❖

I see from the news that domestic abuse is on the increase, and victims are encouraged to dial 999 and follow by dialling a code, 55. This is to alert the police that you are in need of immediate help. As my wife insists that I bathe in

MUSINGS FROM A PANDEMIC

bleach and Dettol every time I enter the house, I am in real danger of melting.

I tried to call 999 and use the code 55 to report this, but found it difficult to call for help as my fingers have dissolved.

Day 15
STAY OFF MY STICKY TAPE!

7th April 2020

During my visit to my local supermarket to buy essentials (mostly beer), I waited at the checkout which had the shortest queue. This happened to be the "ten items or less" line.

Obediently standing on my piece of tape proving that I was two metres away from the shopper in front of me, who was counting the items in his basket to ensure that he only had ten items or less (everyone does this), my mind drifted to my own shopping basket. Does my six-pack of beer qualify as one item or six? If it counts as six items, what about the bunch of grapes in my basket and the carton with a dozen eggs? Not to mention the super-large bag of nuts to go with my beer. There must be hundreds in there.

While considering if I should move to a more suitable checkout, I felt my neck getting warm. I looked around and there was a chap who had been breathing down my neck. He'd completely ignored his bit of sticky tape on the floor and had invaded mine. So, I took a step forward. He followed.

The checkout operator yelled at me, "Two metres apart!"

I tried to explain that it wasn't my fault, but not wishing to be a tell-tale, I took a step back and trod on his toes. He yelled and dropped his basket, contents rolling around on the floor. I did a quick count. He shouldn't have been in this line anyway as he had loads more than ten items in his basket.

※ ※ ※

Coronavirus myths: one of the common myths surrounding coronavirus is that eating large quantities of garlic will protect you. After extensive scientific research in the best universities in the world, and studies released by the World Health Organisation, there is absolute proof that eating garlic will ensure that people will stay at least two metres away from you.

Going to try this next time when I stand in the ten items or less queue.

Holding your breath while near someone else is supposed to help. I did try that once when I was waiting to be let into the supermarket. Didn't work very well, though, as I turned blue, passed out and lost my place in the queue.

It's been suggested that cow urine can help protect you. I have to ask how anyone could have arrived at this conclusion. My theory is that one of the loons currently trying to sabotage the new 5G network lives near a farm, tried to milk a cow but extracted the wrong liquid. Having found out he preferred that to milk, he recommended it to his friends, so the myth continues.

Another popular myth is that you can protect yourself by drinking alcohol regularly. I was really disappointed to see this one has been disproved as I've been using this as an excuse since the lockdown began.

The government has advised that you should keep your cat inside as they may be able to bring the virus in on their fur. It has been proved that cats cannot catch the human form of coronavirus, so you should be fairly safe as long as you don't eat one.

Washing hands is still essential as it has been proved that coronavirus is a respiratory illness which enters your body through your nose or mouth, and perhaps eyes, as the scientific community are still unsure if the virus can enter through other bodily orifices.

So, I have also taken to washing my hands *before* I visit the toilet. You never know.

Day 16

JEHOVAH'S WITNESSES WERE RIGHT ALL ALONG

8th April 2020

Extinction Rebellion have cancelled their planned demonstration. They had scheduled a mass protest in London on 23 May to call for action on tackling the climate crisis. This protest was arranged to cause the most amount of disruption possible and timed for the start of the UK bank holiday and FA Cup final.

However, their future plan of trying to close off Heathrow Airport has been postponed; they need at least a few aircraft to land as due to the panic buying of lentils, the shops have run out. As lentils don't grow in this country, we have to wait for new stock to arrive from the US, so they are getting a bit hungry.

Also, the executive committee of Extinction Rebellion have emerged from their weed-induced coma just long enough to realise that there would be no point in the protest anyway as there is no traffic in London any more, so nobody would notice if it went ahead. They have worked out that if they glued themselves to the top of a Tube train again, nobody would care and they would probably be there until Christmas.

The group suggested that they would be making "alternative, creative plans for May and June". This will probably involve smoking more weed and a full, frank discussion on how to further their plan to bust us all back to the Stone Age.

Jehovah's Witnesses are celebrating as they think that they've been right all along. They are now delightedly telling us that we are all doomed and it's God's punishment. The Four Horses of the Apocalypse are on the way to spread mayhem and disruption to the world (staying at least two metres apart at all times). They have really been looking forward to this.

According to them it fulfils one of their doomsday predictions. The downside is that there will be no more doors to knock on as they will be living in caves eating squirrels like the rest of us. But they will have a very smug look on their faces.

God is up there, sitting on his throne in heaven, looking down on us, and booms out: "Nothing to do with me. I didn't tell you to eat bats. They are definitely not kosher."

I think I had better pop out to the supermarket quickly to get a few essentials (mostly beer) before Armageddon arrives.

MUSINGS FROM A PANDEMIC

Last week the government announced that it had ordered 17.5 million Covid-19 antibody tests. These tests can screen for whether someone has recovered from the virus. The only slight problem is that they don't work. As the common cold is a type of coronavirus, most of us have had a cold so will likely show positive. These kits are now being offered by sellers in the UK.

I got one cheap on eBay. So far, it has told me that I have definitely had some form of coronavirus in my life, my sugar level is okay, but the bad news is that I'm pregnant.

Day 17
HEINEKEN. REFRESHES THE PARTS OTHER BEERS CANNOT REACH

9th April 2020

We have been commanded by the government that we can only go out once a day for a short walk and visit the supermarket for essential items only.

What is an essential item? As far as I know, we could survive on just bread and water for a short period. Most of us have a tap for water, and we can make our own bread if we could find some flour. So, the police are now threatening to use their sweeping new powers to inspect your supermarket trolley.

As someone who feels guilty when I stand in the ten items or less checkout with eleven things, I think that we should be given at least some idea of what is considered to be essential. For me, it's mostly beer; for others, it may be a multipack of Mars Bars and a bottle of Tango. Apparently, ignorance of the law is no excuse, but complying with the rules is going to be almost impossible if we don't know what the rules are.

Once the government has its way and tells us what we can eat, when, and what quantity, we can then look for some cunning ways to sidestep the new regulations and still try to get what we want. This is going to be really difficult as the next step is likely to be the repurposing of airport customs officers who are not working because there are no flights.

Supermarket exits will be changed from sliding glass doors to red and green channels where these customs officers cast their beady eyes over each exiting customer, picking out the shiftier ones who they suspect have too many toilet rolls or other contraband that makes our lives worth living. Once the X-ray machines are installed and sniffer dogs posted at all exits, it's going to be like sneaking in that extra bottle of duty-free at the end of our annual fortnight in Torremolinos.

Those were the days.

I was running a little short of my blood pressure medication. Us old farts always have something wrong with us. So tried my GP surgery but couldn't get through on the phone.

Decided to call a private clinic that I have used before to get hold of a prescription.

"Yes, of course," they told me, "but you have to pop in for a blood pressure check first."

Sounds reasonable, I thought.

Essential journey so should be okay. Arrived at the clinic. Blood pressure checked. Seemed fine.

"Can I have my prescription now?" I asked.

"When was your last blood test?" asked the doctor, then added, "And have you ever had your prostate checked?"

I didn't like where this was going. Went into a small room with what looked like a dentist's chair with arm pads. A young nurse stabbed my arm and withdrew loads of blood. I wasn't really concentrating as my mind was on the next imminent procedure. Having never had my prostate checked and only a vague idea of where it was, I was getting a little nervous.

I've been violated! He was rummaging up there for ages, talking to me at the same time.

"I see you live in Dunstable," he said. "There is a good kebab shop there."

"You can tell all that from one finger?" I asked.

After his enthusiastic examination, he found everything where it should be, correct size and correct number of bits.

He must have had long fingers. I've had a sore throat since and a strange taste in my mouth. All this for £250. I should have charged him more. After my degrading and humiliating experience, I was told that everything was absolutely fine and no worries.

I was sent next door to see his secretary to ask for M4510. Assuming this was a vitamin supplement, I went ahead and agreed. When I got home a quick Google search to see which medication he had advised as it didn't seem to be on the prescription.

M4510 is not a vitamin! It's a sneaky code that only doctors can understand. But Google spilled the beans. It is a procedure to stick a tube and camera up my pee hole into my bladder because his finger wouldn't fit. This is to have a rummage around of the bits he couldn't reach last time.

I phoned his secretary and cancelled that one.

Going to have a lie-down as the cushions on my favourite chair are not thick enough. Might have a beer first, though, as it is a medical essential – tried sweet tea, but it didn't hit the spot.

After all, Heineken really can refresh the parts other beers cannot reach.

Day 18

A DIFFERENT WAY OF GREETING

10th April 2020

Due to the continued rise of coronavirus, many things in life have changed, one being the methods used to greet each other, which have altered probably forever.

A kiss on the cheek to say hello? Not any more.

A handshake to greet a friend or colleague? No longer an acceptable form of communication or introduction. These days we just tend to wave at each other from a distance before continuing on our way. Social skills learned over generations of human evolution have melted away in a matter of weeks, leaving us feeling awkward and confused as to the polite way to say hello.

As social creatures we have, through trial and error over the last few thousand years, evolved polite and civilised methods of proving that we are not a threat to each other. This may involve a smile, although showing our teeth can be interpreted as aggression. A kiss will mean that I have allowed you into my space and don't feel threatened by you. A handshake shows that I am using my sword hand to greet you, so I'm not an enemy.

We must look to develop different social skills in the future. As I watched my dogs meeting their friends in the park, I took a greater than usual interest in their method of communication and greeting. This usually starts with two dogs approaching each other; they form a little circle and commence to sniff each other's bottoms. Their tails start to wag. Then off they go to meet someone else. In these few short seconds, they have worked out who it is, that they are no threat, what they had for breakfast, and have caught up on all the local news and their plans for tomorrow, all while boosting their immune system. In effect, they have politely greeted each other and had a nice conversation that would have taken us ages, with the added bonus that nobody has ever caught coronavirus from an arse. (Well, not that sort of arse, but the point still stands.)

I am not suggesting that we should adopt this new form of greeting immediately, as initially it may be slow to catch on. But in future times it could be combined with other forms of greeting practised by primates which involve grooming and sharing tasty parasites picked off each other's bodies. People that voted for the Brexit Party in the last election (and formerly the National Front) have been using this as a form of greeting for years.

※ ※ ※

On this subject I am delighted to report that since my post last week mentioning Brexit, I have had some really interesting feedback. Suggestions have been made about where I can stick my opinion, assuring me that the big red thing in the photo was not really suggesting that we will give 350 million pounds a week to the NHS.

It's called a bus, and it did. So there!

Another philosophical individual reminded me that "Brexit Means Brexit" and "We have left already and there's no going back".

I replied, "Please keep up and focus. That post was days ago; there've been lots more since. Please get down from that electrical pylon, it's not a 5G mast. All you are going to do is turn everyone's lights off, probably starting with yours. Or you could stay up there for the view of the greener grass on the other side of the fence. Don't think that you will ever taste it, though."

I would be most grateful for more feedback as it's nice to know I'm making an impression.

Day 19

BOOST YOUR IMMUNE SYSTEM

11th April 2020

Spent most of yesterday arguing with Alexa.

Difficult to have a deep and meaningful discussion with a little round box, but I was bored. I asked her to give me her opinion on the current coronavirus outbreak in the UK and likely prognosis on when the lockdown measures will be lifted.

"What would you like to play?" was her reply.

Too complicated, I thought. So tried again.

"Alexa, when will the lockdown end?"

"Playing 'Monster Mash' by Bobby Pickett and the Crypt-Kickers."

"Shut up," I yelled.

No response.

"Alexa, shut up."

Still no response.

This continued for a few more hours. Me asking questions and her playing more obscure music. So I gave up, unplugged her, and went to pick a fight with Siri instead.

Coronavirus lingers in the air longer than previously thought and spreads further, scientists warn. This unwelcome news that coronavirus can hang around in supermarket air for who knows how long will certainly extend the queues. Apparently, if someone sneezes or coughs in the bread aisle, the virus cloud could contaminate someone buying more beer in the next one. It might be worth considering closing off the bread aisle for a while. We have to be careful.

MUSINGS FROM A PANDEMIC

More news is emerging on the benefits of masturbation during lockdown. A sample scientific study of people who admitted this practice revealed that masturbation increases white blood cell count and thereby increases your immunity to disease. If so inclined, the best place to practise this is at home. Please don't do it during your one daily walk in the park as it will probably frighten the wildlife and get you arrested for standing still for too long. Supermarkets are probably not an appropriate venue, either, as you still may get arrested and lose your place in the queue.

This new revelation fully explains the panic buying of toilet rolls and Kleenex. We all thought that they were being wasted on bottoms. We had no idea that they were assisting in keeping the population healthy and more resistant to disease. Amazon has reported that not only have they run out of toilet paper, tissues and rubbing alcohol, they are now running low on socks.

As no new porn movies are being made due to social distancing measures, it may be worth downloading your inspiration quickly, as when this gets out, the world's porn sites will crash as their servers will have melted. There is absolutely no truth in the myth that masturbation makes you get hairy ears and go blind. This is just a myth propagated by less enlightened, pure and innocent people like myself who do not indulge in this dirty and degrading self-abuse. I have to stop typing now as the screen has gone all fuzzy and I think I've gone deaf.

I would like to propose that in the interests of keeping your family healthy for the good of the country, please observe government advice. Stay at home and dedicate several hours to boosting your immune system today.

Day 20
YOU NEVER KNOW WHO'S WATCHING

12th April 2020

Things are getting really tight out there. The police are out in numbers stopping you from doing anything that makes life worth living. I popped out yesterday for some essential shopping (mostly beer). On my way to my favourite supermarket, I had to pass a police checkpoint. The young officer wandered up to my car window.

"Where are you going, sir?" he asked.

While trying to put on an innocent expression, I was quickly calculating how to reply, thinking it unwise to tell him about my true purpose for breaking the curfew. My mind was working overtime trying to think of essential shopping that would justify me leaving the safety of my prison.

Then an idea struck. "I'm going to my nearest supermarket to buy essential supplies and will only get pasta," I smugly announced.

The young police officer laughed and said, "You won't find any of that in the supermarket, it's all gone now."

Undeterred, I carried on. "Toilet rolls?"

He just gave me a sympathetic smile.

"Rice?"

He shook his head. I was beginning to feel like I was stuck in the Monty Python Cheese Shop sketch. "How about flour and yeast?"

He smiled again and looked at me, obviously assuming I was a little senile and beginning to feel sorry for me. "You haven't asked about bread yet." The police officer was clearly tempting me.

"Is it worth my while?" I asked, expecting the answer to be no.

"Might be," he replied.

Okay. I was getting desperate now, so I adopted a puppy dog expression and looked in his eyes. It was time to play my last card. "How about bread?" I suggested. That seemed to work.

Barriers opened, machine gun towers stood down and dogs were called away.

Then, just before he waved me through, he dipped in his pocket and produced a ten-pound note.

Passed it through the car window and asked, "While you're at the supermarket getting your beers, can you get some for me and drop them off on the way back?"

※ ※ ※

We have to be really careful now. There is a network of collaborators and informers in our midst. Sympathisers are peering at us through partially closed curtains, reporting how many shopping bags we bring home and informing the authorities on how many walks we are taking. Peeping at us all with binoculars and rummaging through our recycling bins to record how many old beer cans and chocolate wrappers are contained within. They are recording our every move to pass on to the appropriate department, hoping to have their annoying neighbour shot by the authorities as they still bear a grudge because you parked on their driveway last year and play music too loud.

We know who you are. Come the liberation, the sympathisers will be rounded up and made to stand in the park while we all shout "Tell-tale tit" in a loud voice before getting back to our usual mundane neighbourly squabbles. I think I will have a daily barbecue of old lorry tyres that need burning, and am considering organising a pop concert in my garden to celebrate our release.

Now that the roads are completely empty of traffic, motorways are beginning to look like disused airfields and the government has ceased all roadworks. This is mostly because this national pastime of pissing off motorists and causing gridlocked traffic is no longer any fun as there is no one left on the roads to piss off. Traffic cone manufacturers are really suffering, the firms that make temporary traffic lights are in desperate trouble, and radio traffic announcers are starving. However, speed cameras are still working so they're getting their priorities right – they need the money to pay the traffic wardens. Local authorities are eagerly waiting for the traffic to return to normal so an even larger scale programme of disruption can be commenced.

Day 21

PLEASE, BORIS

13th April 2020

China just upgraded the status of dogs from "livestock" to "pets". This will also include cats, bats, cockroaches, starfish, rats, snakes, and seahorses on sticks. Therefore, in line with current regulations, the

Wuhan branch of Pet City is permitted to re-open as it has now been reclassified as a supermarket.

※ ※ ※

Due to the closure of all pubs in this country, the beer stored in their cellars is now passing its sell-by date and is beginning to go off. This is a tragic waste. I think the time has come for a partial and temporary lifting of the lockdown so that these barrels can be rolled out into the car park as a reward for our good behaviour. Please, Boris. I know you are feeling better.

Please, Boris. I know I didn't vote for you, but we have all been good and obedient and have stayed at home when commanded. We have only gone out for one walk a day and only to the shops for essential supplies (mostly beer). We have endeavoured to comply with all government advice and assisted our fellow humans by building up our immunity by only engaging in government-sanctioned self-abuse at home and not in the park or supermarket, thereby protecting the NHS.

Please, Boris. We can all form an orderly line outside the pub, glass in hand. I promise to stand at least two metres away from anyone else. I promise not to sneeze, cough, or block the pavement while waiting. I will even bring my own glass.

Please, Boris. Do this for your country. Please, Boris. I promise to vote for you in the next election (maybe) if you do this for us. That way we can all get shitfaced at least once before returning to our prisons ...

※ ※ ※

Extra weight has been added to the theory that 5G causes coronavirus. David Icke, the well-known headbanger and renowned loony, is telling anyone who will listen that coronavirus was actually created by Israel to test their 5G technology. This is probably good news as David Icke is well known to be as mad as a box of frogs and will likely have the opposite effect of discounting this conspiracy theory for ever, as even the most stupid of 5G-tower-climbing morons will have to think again and reconsider their actions.

David Icke's other well-known theories include the likelihood that the royal family are actually lizards and the world is controlled by reptiles.

I would certainly not agree that *all* the

royal family are lizards. But he may have a point about reptiles ruling the world as there is a poisonous orange one currently infesting the White House. Attempts by pest controllers to lure it out using cheeseburgers and UV light have not resulted in success. Although this creature has the IQ of a paving slab, its finely tuned animal instinct is that of a sewer rat, so it has managed to evade capture up until now. This particularly toxic, thin-skinned specimen is known to be sniffing around the White House at night when the lights are off, looking for big red buttons to press and sending poisonous tweets with its webbed feet.

It only emerges into daylight to spit venom at journalists and White House staff before scurrying back into the safety of its nest behind the skirting board in the Oval Office. Other members of this dangerous species have been used in a more productive way by Amazonian tribes, who dip their darts and arrows in them.

This shows that if not infesting the White House, it could at least be useful.

More info tomorrow. Unless Boris agrees to my tearful begging. If so, I might have a day off.

Day 22
BREAKING NEWS

14th Date 2020

Boris Johnson's senior adviser Dominic Cummings has returned to work at Downing Street after showing symptoms of coronavirus over a fortnight ago.

Asked whether Mr Cummings was back at work, a spokesman said on Tuesday: "Correct. The real prime minister is back in Number Ten running the country today."

Boris is beginning his journey of recovery at Chequers, where he is not working or receiving official papers in his red boxes and has not had any telephone calls with the Queen or Dominic Cummings. Instead, he is keeping his head down in case anyone asks a difficult question.

Reported in *The Guardian* today. Man accidentally ejects himself from fighter jet during flight. Sixty-four-year-old lands in field after grabbing ejection handle to steady himself. French air accident investigators found this chap unhurt, still strapped into the aircraft seat.

He had heard that the French version of Costco had received a new delivery of toilet rolls, and didn't want to miss out. So he decided to get there as quickly as possible. However, as the jet approached the store, it did not seem to be slowing down, so he decided to pull the handbrake. As he was not fully conversant with the workings of a military jet, or basic aerodynamics, he was surprised to find himself floating in mid-air, watching as the jet departed to pick up another toilet-roll-seeking pensioner.

This was the first in a spate of recent near misses as air traffic control are reporting that there has been a recent increase in old people with parachutes causing disruption to airport flight paths, trying to beat the panic buying. So it does seem to be catching on. Idiots.

Anyway, just off to the airport as I've heard that Tesco's in the Outer Hebrides has just received a consignment of toilet rolls and pasta. While I'm there I might pick up some other essentials (mostly beer).

Just found out why the queues at supermarkets are so long. Visited my local store today. Only took a small basket as I didn't need much. Got to the checkout. A spotty youth peered at me through his protective Perspex screen.

"Want a bag?" he asked.

"How much is it?" I replied. This seemed to confuse him.

He pressed his intercom button to ask his supervisor the price of carrier bags. "Ten pence." I agreed.

He tried to scan the first item. Till wouldn't read the code. This obviously confused him as he tried again and again with the same result. After a few minutes waiting and the queue building up behind me, I remembered that I needed some cheese. So I quickly rushed to the chiller display and ran back. He was still trying to scan the same item.

Then I remembered dog food. So rushed over to the dog food section and grabbed a bag. He had given up trying to scan the item and was inputting the code manually. Five minutes later I remembered that I was running low on milk. So rushed over to the dairy section and grabbed a bottle and ran back. He was still trying to input the code without success. By this time, an even longer line of exasperated shoppers was building up behind me.

This supermarket operates a one in, one out system, so the queue outside was now extending up the road and around the block. While I was still waiting for him to scan the second item, I continued to grab some more forgotten items until I had filled another four baskets. By now I was feeling both embarrassed for myself and sorry for the dopey kid trying to work out the checkout system, so I suggested that if he could open the self-checkout, I would scan it myself. He gratefully agreed and was glad to get rid of me.

I self-scanned the first item. A robotic voice announced, "Unknown item in bagging area." After another fifteen minutes fighting with that checkout, I finally escaped. I think the spotty youth and the self-checkout are related.

Trump has again shocked the world. He has now withdrawn funding from the WHO, the only independent organisation that is trying to protect us. This is mainly to direct attention from his pitiful response to coronavirus with his usual trick of blaming someone else for his cock-ups while trying to gain more votes from the hillbillies that elected him in the first place. Deep South Republican voters were so horrified that the virus seems to have originated though the Chinese eating bats, they almost choked on their rattlesnake, possum and raccoon gumbo. It also put them off their alligator and catfish ice cream.

Trump has now announced that he will deal with Covid-19 himself, and has tweeted that coronavirus is incredible, and happy virus day to you all.

Day 23

MOTORWAY GRAND PRIX

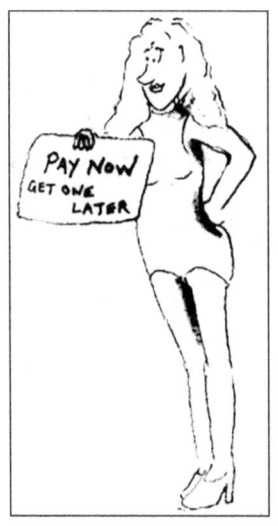

15th April 2020

Had to go to work yesterday. As I run a small business, I do still have to wander into the office occasionally to brush away the cobwebs and water the plants. Currently all my staff are furloughed. That is, all except me. As a company director who relies on dividends to be able to eat, I seem to have fallen through the gaps and will not receive any government help.

No problem, I can always eat the office plants. Will save me watering them. Next on the menu will probably be the cobwebs.

Driving along the empty motorway at normal old-man speed, hogging the middle lane, I was quite enjoying the rare privilege of being out of my isolation. Then up ahead I saw a rare sight. Queued cars and lorries with hazard lights flashing. I joined the line, expecting the traffic to start moving soon. Two hours later, still sitting in the queue, I was starting to get bored. Other drivers had left their vehicles and were using their government-controlled one walk a day to stretch their legs and sunbathe on their bonnets, only interrupted by police sirens and fire engines speeding up the hard shoulder. Obviously, there was another accident up ahead.

In the past few weeks, there has been an increase in serious accidents on motorways. This is mostly because drivers have never had the chance to drive on the M25 faster than 20 mph and are not used to it. Now they see an empty road ahead of them and blood rushes to their heads. Believing themselves to be indestructible racing drivers, they are taking this opportunity to kill themselves.

Unfortunately, most crashes involve the hitting of someone else – usually people like me doing old-man speed while hogging the middle lane. We are frequently surprised to find hot hatchbacks and BMW sports cars wedged in our boot lids.

Formula One is now cancelled for the foreseeable future, and Sky are making it exceedingly difficult for me to cancel my sports package. Being bored to death watching second division football matches beamed live from Azerbaijan and repeats of the 1968 European Cup final, I think the multitude of motorway cameras should be fed live to our Sky boxes. We can then watch these idiots trying to kill themselves in real time, while safely self-isolating away from the roads in the comfort of our own home, drinking more beer.

MUSINGS FROM A PANDEMIC

❋ ❋ ❋

News today that California governor Gavin Newsom sent shockwaves through the West Coast on Thursday when he officially ordered all 40 million of the state's residents to shelter in place (meaning stay home unless buying necessities or seeking medical care). But among the "essential services" that he deemed would remain open were pharmacies, food stores, and shops selling weed.

On the subject of essential services, prostitutes in Amsterdam's famous red zone are suffering as these workers do not have a fixed income, they don't receive paid sick leave, and lack savings to fall back on when they're not on their backs. Some of these inventive workers have launched a crowdfunding appeal. Others are advertising a special offer that if you pay now, you can come later.

An alarming report received from hospitals concerns the excessive use of do-not-resuscitate orders. As an older person but not yet too doddery, I am getting a bit worried that this may not be confined to hospitals but used elsewhere in the community. I was due to visit the chiropodist tomorrow for essential toenail maintenance and have my dentures polished on

Monday. I was also planning to pop down to the supermarket later for some essential supplies (mostly beer) but scared that I might fall asleep in the queue. Just to be safe, I think I will stay at home for a couple of days and protect myself from the NHS.

Day 24

DAILY WALK FOR SALE

16th April 2020

According to recent studies released from China, during the peak of infections, smokers were less likely to die from coronavirus. I have now been a non-smoker for 6 years, 6 months, 16 days, 9 hours, 25 minutes, and 11 seconds. Not counting, though, and don't miss it at all (much), only every waking moment and sometimes in my sleep.

Although this study does go against every other opinion from scientists throughout the world, it is attractive to an ex-smoker like me who was addicted for years. So, with the new justification, I am considering having a fag. The only thing stopping me is that I still have a little bit of commonsense rattling around in the back of my head somewhere, and it would be a real pain having to wash my hands between puffs.

※ ※ ※

Originally I started writing these posts to cheer up my daughter and a few like-minded friends. But she challenged me to write a new one every day during the lockdown. Although I'm having fun with these, I thought I would use today's to spill the beans.

My daughter, being somewhat sedentary and a Facebook enthusiast, normally only exercises her fingers. She normally confines herself to one walk a week. This is usually around Asda, but she always goes early so she can park close to the entrance. She would never consider walking any further than a quick wander around the local charity shop (next to Asda) to buy more tat. So, government advice suggesting that she has been given one walk a day has come as a surprise. As she has no idea how to go out for a walk without buying anything, and the shops being closed, she has no intention of using this gift. Not wishing to waste this good fortune, she has decided to sell her one walk a day on eBay.

So far, the bidding has been lively and has reached a decent sum. I think that this may be taking advantage of the government's kind offer, but at least it won't go to waste.

※ ※ ※

Now McDonald's and Kentucky Fried Chicken are planning to reopen for takeaways. The staff at these outlets are busy opening kitchens, clearing out the fridges and changing the oil in the fryers. They don't need to clean the windows as they are receiving a daily licking from fast-food devotees hanging around outside trying to taste the remnants of last month's offerings.

My local pub has really clean windows. I know that because I always hopefully try the door during my daily walk. I think I tasted a hint of Guinness on their window yesterday.

※ ※ ※

New guidelines are emerging from the police on what we can do during the lockdown. This includes permission to attend a supermarket once a week, and going out to buy tools to mend a fence, but only if it was damaged by bad weather. Sitting down during your walk is also banned. We are not allowed to go out to buy brushes and paint to redecorate the kitchen – still seems okay to paint the hallway and living room though. Definitely going to use this excuse to get out of doing the decorating. Every cloud has a silver lining.

Day 25

A LITTLE MORE SERIOUS TODAY

17th April 2020

As my wife is Greek, we are now celebrating the Orthodox Easter. This usually comes a week or two after our holiday period. Yesterday being Holy Friday, I was allowed to sit unmolested in the living room without becoming collateral damage during her bi-hourly online Zumba class. All was eerily quiet, no loud Latino music, just the sound of birds in the garden and the gentle patter of raindrops on the window while she observed the long traditions of her religion.

We normally go to Greece for Easter, but due to the lockdown and ban on travel we are staying at home this year. All churches in Greece are closed, so for the first time in their lives, people have to watch the services on TV and not take part in this countrywide annual event. As Easter is the most important annual celebration for Greeks all over the world, they have retained this tradition as part of their cultural heritage, which has gone unchanged for many decades. When we first got together as a couple, I decided to become fully involved. This is now part of our family life.

In Greece it's the main holiday of the year. A full four-day festival which plays out the sadness of loss, the contemplation of life and the celebration of rebirth.

Every family cooks a whole lamb to celebrate. Normally, when in Greece we do the same. But this year will be a little different. Unless I can use my daily walk for a little sheep rustling at the local farm, we may be stuck with a banquet of fish fingers and a red egg. Never mind, there is always next year.

In my opinion, this beats the hell out of a

hot cross bun and a chocolate Easter egg. Even if there are a few bunny rabbits around. We do need to look back on the loss of our own culture and reflect on the meaning of our lives in these most difficult of times. Some traditions bond us and should be shared. I have adopted this way of life and hope that after reading this you can in some way do the same.

Back to my normal style tomorrow as we still need to laugh.

Day 26

THE TESTS ARE FALLING FAR SHORT

18th April 2020

Earlier this month, the British government announced that they would be testing 100,000 people per day for coronavirus. So far, the tests are falling well short. The government is having a dilemma. Normally, they would quote any figure that comes into their head as no one will check anyway. But this time, they are being watched, so they need to come up with an inventive way of massaging the figures. Perhaps they need to write them on the side of a bus. Lots of people fell for that one.

There are 27 testing centres in total and there are reports of some people having to drive hundreds of miles to reach their nearest site. The government says there is capacity to do about 40,000 tests a day across the UK, but only about 20,000 tests are being processed, as the government in its wisdom has strategically placed the testing stations to ensure nobody can get to them. It would have made more sense to put these in hospital car parks as they are empty because no one is allowed to visit relatives. But this requires logical thought, and common sense has never been involved in any previous policy, so why start now?

One of the new testing centres is in the car park of Ikea. It would at least be worth considering the long drive if the store was open too. At least you could get a bit of cheap flatpack furniture as a lockdown project to keep the kids amused for a couple of weeks.

PETER BARBER

Had to go to my office this morning to make sure it is still there. Thought I would combine the trip with a visit to the supermarket for weekly essentials (mostly beer). Driving along the M1 motorway, past the fossilised traffic cones with nobody digging, in the temporary 40 mph speed limit enforced by average-speed cameras, I noticed how difficult it was to keep to the speed limit with nothing in front of or behind me. My mind kept drifting off and my speed slowly increased until I suddenly remembered the limit and slowed right down to well below the enforced speed, thereby getting back down below the average.

Speeding fines must now be keeping the economy afloat as there has been a drastic drop in crime in this country. Shoplifters have become unemployed as all the shops are shut. Boozed-up yobbos aren't wreaking havoc at night on the way to the kebab shop as the pubs are closed and the kebab shop will only deliver. The police are trying to find something to keep them occupied. So realising that they only need about 10 per cent of the force to stop us doing anything that makes life worth living, the other

90 per cent have been put on traffic duty (although there is no traffic) by using incognito cars to catch speeding motorists.

Gone are the brightly coloured vehicles of the past; they have been cunningly disguised as normal cars to lull you into a false sense of security. Assuming these innocent-looking motorists are doing the same as you and going about normal business, it soon becomes clear that they are not one of us. Blue lights previously hidden behind the radiator grill start flashing as they stop you to dish out another fine to screw up your day.

But I have news for you.

While you were chasing motorists in your unmarked car, doing 31 mph in a 30-mph road, you have completely missed the evidence right under your nose. Have you not wondered about people self-isolating together who don't actually like each other? Put this together with the compelling evidence that Amazon Prime has run out of shovels and freezers. Neighbours reporting that the chap next door has suddenly developed a taste for gardening at 3 a.m. in the morning. Once the lockdown ends there is likely to be a sudden spike in missing person reports, and sniffer dogs will have to be taken away from airports to smell the ground over the new rose bushes that have become so popular recently.

Popping out now to lock the freezer and hide the lawnmower. Just in case.

Day 27

POSTCARD FROM MY HOLIDAY

19th April 2020

Dear Mum,
    Hope you are well. I am having a lovely time. Wish you were here. It's very quiet but the people seem nice.
    Saw a policeman yesterday who waved at

me. Not picked up the local lingo yet, but he seemed to be encouraging me to keep walking and said something about not sitting on that rock as there are much nicer things to see further on. I don't think the locals like each other much though. They seem to keep away from each other and cross the road when they see other people approaching. I haven't seen anyone shake hands or greet each other yet. This must be a local tradition.

The food seems nice, but I'm not really used to this foreign stuff. They tend to use quite a lot of oil and make it a bit greasy. Had a bit of tummy trouble yesterday, but you must expect a little of this when on holiday and not used to new things. In keeping with most foreign destinations, they can't make good tea. Luckily, I packed some Tetley tea bags in my suitcase, just in case.

There are no toilet rolls in my bathroom. Perhaps this is another local custom and they have other ways of cleaning themselves. No problem, though, as I have a jumbo pack in my other suitcase. Lucky I booked self-catering. There are no restaurants or bars open. No gift shops selling the usual tourist tat. But I have found a local pharmacy that sells Imodium if I need some.

MUSINGS FROM A PANDEMIC

Found a local supermarket today. I was running out of a few essentials (mostly beer). They have this strange practice of making you stand outside and queue up on red lines painted on the floor. These lines are two metres apart and you are not allowed to cross one until the one in front is empty. This is a bit like box junctions on the roads back home. Not wishing to offend the locals, I complied with this strange rule. When my turn to enter the shop came, I was handed a tissue which seemed to be soaked in alcohol. Not really speaking the language, I indicated that I didn't want any yet as it was a bit early for me. The shop worker insisted, so I took one and put it in my pocket to suck on later.

Once inside the supermarket, I took a look around. It's nice to visit these places in foreign lands to see different and exotic foodstuffs; it's all part of a holiday for me. I did notice that they didn't sell toilet paper, which confirmed my suspicion that it must be a cultural difference. I was a little disappointed to see that most of the items on the shelves were the same as at home. But there didn't seem to be any soap, no handwash, and they obviously didn't like baking in this country as they didn't sell flour or yeast.

After my wander around this quaint little shop, I arrived at the checkout. A similar system to outside was being implemented here. I had to stand on my bit of red tape to wait for the shopper in front of me to clear his bit before I could approach. I was getting the hang of this now. Putting my beer on the checkout, I moved forward to be confronted by a lady sitting in a Perspex box at her till. She scanned my items and pointed at the screen displaying the amount. I did a quick calculation and offered her a local banknote.

She refused to touch my money and pointed at a small machine with buttons on it. I persisted; she again refused my money. I finally realised that this was a free shop. I didn't have to pay for my beer. What a lovely place for a holiday!

On the way out, a local policeman offered to carry my shopping for me and insisted on giving me a lift back to my apartment. Not very impressed with his car, though; there are no windows, only bars. I might invite him in for a beer when we get home to say thank you.

Seriously, Urgent Health Update

Don't usually write any more than one post a day. Nowadays, I seem to have the attention span of a goldfish. But have to share this.

Australian doctors have revealed that it may be possible to spread coronavirus with a fart. Studies have shown that patients with coronavirus show evidence of the virus in their poo. We used to have to cover a fart with a cough, then cover a cough with a fart. Now we have to cover a fart with a cough again and only if wearing a mask. The question is: which end does the mask go?

As only common people fart, it does not apply to me. However, I think social distancing in supermarkets should be increased to five metres just in case, and takeaway curries should be added to the list of banned non-essentials.

Day 28
TURKISH DELIGHT

20th April 2020

MUSINGS FROM A PANDEMIC

Since the start of the coronavirus pandemic, government advice has always been, and still is, that facemasks are not necessary and will not help to protect you against the virus. Yeah? Try telling that to the NHS workers risking their lives every moment of every day. Ask them to work in the ward with no protection.

News that 84 tons of PPE was coming from Turkey on Sunday was announced on Saturday. This didn't turn up. The RAF fell for it and sent a plane to collect the consignment. This was news to the Turks. The first they knew about it was when they asked why a British RAF warplane had just landed at Istanbul airport and were told it was there to collect a delivery.

The Turks checked their dispatch notes, had a quick look in the warehouse and couldn't find the box. They finally gave the Brits a call to ask who ordered it and when. A furious exchange of buck-passing occurred in the British government, bureaucrats swearing that they told someone else to order it as they were on a tea break. Cries of "Not my fault" bounced around Whitehall; internal enquiries being arranged, quangos being set up to investigate, a high court judge appointed to oversee, memos being sent to other bureaucrats before getting lost in the accumulation ribbon of red tape, never to be seen again.

This was until the tea lady assumed responsibility and called her friend at the local kebab shop who called his brother in Istanbul who knew someone in the local factory, thereby sorting out the mess. The Turks have now assembled the order but won't let the plane take off until the cheque clears.

Anyway, I have drifted off the subject.

The main reasons that the government is not advising the general population to wear masks are: first, nobody can get any, and second, the already damaged economy would plummet still further. As a mask covers most of your face, there would no longer be any need to make an effort. Lipstick and cosmetic suppliers are already suffering. Teeth whitening kits are no longer required. Cosmetic surgeons found that Botox and lip fillers have suffered their biggest ever decline, and people that offer nose and lip piercing are seeing the bottom falling out of their business, as the wearers of exotic nose rings will no longer be able to frighten children, so no point, and the lip studs snag the masks.

MUSINGS FROM A PANDEMIC

Finally, I just found out that oil prices have gone into negative. This means that the producers will pay you to take it away. As soon as I heard about this, I popped out to my driveway to start my car and let it tick over for a few hours. Later, I am off to the petrol station to fill up and make a bit of hard cash. I can then walk away with a small profit, a full tank of free fuel, and a few essentials (mostly beer).

Hoping that my electricity suppliers will follow suit. If so, I can leave all my lights on and start my washing machine for one sock at a time. I could make a fortune.

Day 29

NOW ONE FOR THE CHILDREN

21st April 2020

Once upon a time there was a Big Bad Wolf. He was prowling around the deep, dark woods, looking for his breakfast, when he came across a cave. There inside was Benny the Bat hanging upside down, dreaming about the particularly tasty neck he sucked last night.

As Benny was satisfied and comfortable, he felt so safe he switched off his radar. The Big Bad Wolf crept into the cave and with one bite, gobbled up poor Benny. The Big Bad Wolf had no idea that together with the tasty bat he had also eaten a nasty virus.

Not far away lived an old mother pig who had three little pigs and not enough food to feed them. So, she had sent them out into the world to seek their fortunes. She sat them down to give them the same advice that all mothers give their departing children: always wear clean underpants, as if you get run over, the hospital will undress you and you will be really embarrassed.

She added extremely strict instructions to build their own houses and not visit each other, and to make sure that they washed their trotters in hot water with soap. And most importantly, to stay at home and only go out for essentials (mostly pig swill).

Being naughty little pigs, they chose to forget their mother's advice on clean underpants, social distancing and trotter washing, which, unknown to them, they would come to regret. The first little pig was very lazy. He didn't want to work at all, and he built his house out of straw. The second little pig worked a little bit harder, but he was somewhat lazy too and he built his house out of sticks. Then, they sang and danced and played together the rest of the day. The third little pig worked hard all day and built his house with bricks. It was a sturdy house complete with a fine fireplace and chimney. It looked like it could withstand the strongest of winds.

The Big Bad Wolf, still being hungry because the bat, although very tasty, was not really enough to satisfy him, was looking for more breakfast when he happened to pass by the lane where the Three Little Pigs lived. He saw the straw house, and he could smell the pig inside. He thought the pig would make a mighty fine meal and his mouth began to water.

So he knocked on the door and said: "Little pig! Little pig! Let me in! Let me in!"

But the little pig saw the wolf's big paws through the keyhole, so he answered back: "No! No! No! Not by the hairs on my chinny chin chin!"

The wolf bared his teeth and said: "Then I'll huff and I'll puff and I'll blow your house down." So he huffed, and he puffed, and he blew the house down!

The wolf opened his jaws very wide and bit down as hard as he could, but the first little pig escaped and ran away to hide with the second little pig. This little pig had forgotten his mother's advice on social distancing and forgot to wash his trotters in hot water with soap, and therefore inadvertently spread the newly acquired virus to his brother pig.

The wolf continued down the lane and he passed by the second house made of sticks. He saw the house, and he smelled the pigs inside, and his mouth began to water as he thought about the fine dinner they would make. So he knocked on the door and said: "Little pigs! Little pigs! Let me in! Let me in!"

But the little pigs saw the wolf's pointy ears through the keyhole, so they answered back: "No! No! No! Not by the hairs on our chinny chin chin!"

So the wolf bared his teeth and said: "Then I'll huff and I'll puff and I'll blow your house down!" So he huffed, and he puffed, and he blew the house down!

The wolf was greedy, and he tried to catch both pigs at once. But he was too greedy and got neither! His big jaws clamped down on nothing but air, and the two little pigs scrambled away as fast as their little trotters would carry them. The wolf chased them down the lane and he almost caught them. But they made it to the brick house and slammed the door closed before the wolf could catch them.

As the little pigs did not understand things like virus transmission rates and didn't really comprehend graphs and statistics on infection rates in the community, the Three Little Pigs had no idea that they were carrying the virus which they'd caught by being huffed and puffed on. They knew the wolf wanted to eat them. And that was very, very true. The wolf had only eaten a small bat all day and he had worked up a large appetite chasing the pigs around, and now he could smell all three of them inside and he knew that the Three Little Pigs would make a lovely feast.

So, the wolf knocked on the door and said: "Little pigs! Little pigs! Let me in! Let me in!"

But the little pigs saw the wolf's narrow eyes through the keyhole, so they answered back: "No! No! No! Not by the hairs on our chinny chin chin!"

So the wolf bared his teeth and said: "Then I'll huff and I'll puff and I'll blow your house down." Well! He huffed and he puffed. He puffed and he huffed. And he huffed, huffed, and he puffed, puffed. But he could not blow the house down.

At last, he was so out of breath that he couldn't huff and he couldn't puff any more because he was beginning to get a slight fever and a dry cough. He stopped to rest and thought a bit. This was too much. The wolf danced about with rage and swore he would come down the chimney and eat up the little pig for his supper. But while he was climbing onto the roof, the little pig made up a blazing fire and put a big pot full of water on to boil. Then, just as the wolf was coming down the chimney, the little piggy pulled off the lid – and plop! In fell the wolf into the scalding water.

The little piggy put the lid back on, boiled the wolf up, and the Three Little Pigs ate him for supper, virus and all.

The very next day, Three Little Piggies went to Wuhan market ...

Day 30

ALTERNATIVE MEDICINE

22nd April 2020

China have now allowed the wet markets to reopen. This is to include the wildlife section. After outrage in national and international newspapers, the decision has been vigorously defended by the Chinese and they have informed us that the animals they are selling are not for food but are medicinal.

Apparently, if you eat a pangolin, you develop thick skin and become bulletproof. Fruit bats have been classified as a high-protein vegetable, and civet cats are thought to replace Viagra and have an additional bonus of pooing out coffee beans which you can sell in Harrods. Doctors in Wuhan are claiming success in the fight against coronavirus by prescribing a course of market produce as an alternative to modern medicine, which has had no effect on the virus. "Just take two cockroaches with a roasted scorpion and call me in the morning."

Homeopaths have caught onto the idea. They have a theory that if you take something really bad for you like deadly nightshade, then dilute it hundreds of times until there is no deadly nightshade left, it can cure you of all sorts of illness. Homeopaths are now conducting experiments with bats. If successful, we can forget the vaccination and just pop along to Holland & Barrett for a dose.

I was most upset to receive a message regarding one of my recent posts. I was accused of plagiarising old fairy stories and adapting them for my own use. I wish to object to this scandalous and unjust comment and point out that it is absolutely and categorically true. However, in my defence I am only following government protocol as they started it by adapting fairy tales and writing them on buses.

Other fairy tales that I am thinking of mucking about with include: "The princess who spent her time hopefully kissing toads without observing social distancing rules but has now been locked away for her own protection." "Sleeping Beauty has no chance of being woken up now as Prince Charming is staying at home with his mum and only allowed out to go to the shops." And "The Three Little Piggies who went to market found out that the roast beef they were eating had black wings so panicked and cried 'Wee wee wee' all the way home."

※ ※ ※

Trump has now realised that his support base is in danger of being wiped out. People on the streets in America are holding placards with

"Set Us Free" and "I Want a Haircut". Have seen that one of the people encouraging them to protest has now been "Set Free". He has died from coronavirus.

Realising that if all stupid people stay on the streets protesting, he is going to lose the next election, he is now encouraging only Democrat voters to go out and insisted that anyone who votes Republican must "Stay at home and keep safe".

Day 31

LETTER TO AMERICA

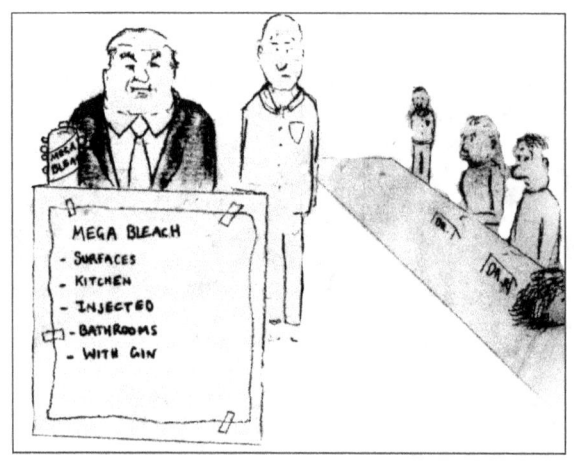

23rd April 2020

In these days of staying at home we have just a few pleasures left to us.
 I saw a pigeon on my windowsill yesterday. Been waiting by the window today in

case it comes back. Watching white puffy clouds pass across the blue sky, listening to the distant sound of breeze in the trees in the park, killing time waiting for the highlight of my day. Trump's daily White House briefing.

I was not disappointed. Trump is suggesting research into whether coronavirus might be treated by injecting disinfectant into the body. He also appeared to propose irradiating patients' bodies with UV light. During Thursday's White House coronavirus task force briefing, an official presented the results of US government research that indicated coronavirus appeared to weaken more quickly when exposed to sunlight and heat.

The study also showed bleach could kill the virus in saliva or respiratory fluids within five minutes, and isopropyl alcohol could kill it even more quickly.

"So, supposing we hit the body with a tremendous – whether it's ultraviolet or just very powerful light," the president said, turning to Dr Deborah Birx, the White House coronavirus response coordinator, "and I think you said that hasn't been checked but you're going to test it. And then I said, supposing you brought the light inside of the body, which you can do either through the skin or in some other way. And I think you said you're going to test that too. Sounds interesting." The president continued. "And then I see the disinfectant where it knocks it out in a minute. One minute. And is there a way we can do something like that, by injection inside or almost a cleaning? So it'd be interesting to check that."

The White House doctor, looking quite uncomfortable by this point, looked at Trump and suggested that it's probably not a good idea to inject bleach into people.

Now he was in full flow, and asked Dr Birx if she had ever heard of using "the heat and the light" to treat coronavirus.

The doctor again looked at Trump with an expression normally reserved to explain things to a particularly stupid child and replied, "Not as a treatment. I mean, certainly, fever is a good thing. When you have a fever it helps your body respond. But I've not seen heat or light."

"I think it's a great thing to look at," Mr Trump said.

Pulmonologist Dr Vin Gupta told NBC News: "This notion of injecting or ingesting any type of cleansing product into the body is irresponsible and it's dangerous. It's a common method that people utilise when they want to kill themselves." Then added, "Don't take medical advice from Trump."

Unknown to Trump, this latest information will erode his voting numbers still further. In the more stupid parts of America, supermarkets have suddenly seen a shortage of bleach, Domestos, and pine-flavoured antiseptic fluid. People being admitted to hospital after eating Christmas tree lights have overtaken coronavirus patients, creating a shortage of ICU beds. That's what happens when you take medical advice from Trump.

※ ※ ※

LETTER TO AMERICA

Dear Americans,

I have a lot of respect for you. I send my blogs using an American-designed phone which is smarter than I will ever be. The United States have succeeded in putting men on the moon, and lead the world in technology. American companies have convinced us to pay five pounds for a coffee and ensured we all believe that McDonald's is a health food. You must be cleverer than you make out. Even though most of you voted for Trump (according to Trump), I do not think you are stupid.

But. When it comes to electing presidents, your track record is disappointing. George W. Bush was not the sharpest tool in the shed. Ronald Reagan was best known for starring in a film with a chimp. And we're not even talking about Nixon, or the one that grew peanuts (mostly between his ears). The only half decent one you had you shot.

But Trump is your best one yet. He is the cherry on top!

I know that we voted for Brexit and Boris. But that was only temporary insanity, and we are feeling better now.

Please think carefully when you cast your vote in November. It's up to you. But as Hollywood has closed its doors and turned the lights out, and America being the leaders in entertainment, you may wish to vote for him anyway just to keep us entertained for another four years.

Day 32

DEAR MR SECRET SERVICE

24th April 2020

Dear Mr Secret Service,
I hope that you are well.
Further to my daily post which was published yesterday on Facebook, I thank you for your email and explanation that the president's comments have been taken out of context and it was only more fake news. I was relieved to read that he was only joking.

I do understand your concern as I shouldn't really be passing on news from BBC, CNN, NBC, the *New York Times* and other fake news providers, so I will be more careful of my sources. In future I will use more credible sources such as the Monster Raving Loony Party and the Flat Earth Society.

As per your request, I have submitted today's redacted version for your consent prior to posting.

Hopefully, this will now meet with your approval.

Please accept my sincere apologies for any offence caused.

And please don't kill me. I promise to be good now.

Love, Peter xx

MORE NEWS

Amazon has now sold out of the new Vibease smart remote control with iPhone & Android via Wi-Fi and Bluetooth (pink). These devices have the ability to share sexual experiences worldwide.

Being an older gentleman, I remember having pen pals, so am keen to try the new updated version. As someone who has never played a computer game, I will need a lot of practice, but my iPhone is currently suffering from a touch of erectile dysfunction since I dropped it in the toilet. I am still wondering how the whole thing works.

Would we be able to use dating sites to meet other people that have them? We could ask for their email address, phone number and Wi-Fi code of their vibrator. We could put these codes on Facebook! See how many friends we can get, and how many likes. If our post goes viral, we wouldn't be able to walk, so wouldn't be able to go out to catch coronavirus or go shopping. So by staying at home, we can protect the NHS.

Divorce rates would skyrocket with people having virtual affairs and virtual sneaky sex with someone in Mombasa while sitting in their living room avoiding getting kicked to death during the wife's daily virtual Zumba lesson.

This device opens up so many possibilities.

Premature ejaculation will be a thing of the past. If you are reaching the end too quickly, just press pause and continue later. Use of the mute button will avoid you getting in trouble with the neighbours, and nobody will have to sleep on the wet patch.

Stupid people that have been spending their time wreaking havoc on 5G transmitters are now back up the tower trying to fix them.

The oldest profession in the world will be no more! And brothels will be converted into phone shops. People have suddenly lost interest in traditional computer games, so Xbox and PlayStation are now rushing to develop their own version. The biggest problem I can see, though, is that the human race will end. This is going to be far too easy. There is no need to send it flowers. You don't need to take it for romantic walks, no candlelight dinners necessary, and you don't even need to send it a Valentine's card.

Amazon is also out of stock of full-size interactive dolls. I have sent an email to the manufacturers to ask if they can reprogram one to make tea, cook my breakfast, and bring me my slippers. But I'm still waiting for their reply. If I get one, I can send it out for essential supplies (mostly beer) while I stay at home and play with my iPhone.

Day 33

INTERVIEW WITH A VIRUS

25th April 2020

The current coronavirus pandemic has changed our lives forever. We have been forced to refocus on the important things and take our attention away from the petty squabbling of the past. The world was in trouble long before anyone had heard of Covid-19. Arguments and counterarguments about Brexit consumed our media and political system for years. Long before the current pandemic, our minds were being poisoned on a daily basis by left- and right-wing media eagerly trying to convince us of the merits of mutual self-destruction while doing their best to reawaken our primitive tribal instinct for divisiveness because we have different opinions. The ugly spectre of racism was disguised and rebranded as national interest and trade deals.

Slowly the world is beginning to heal. We are no longer focusing on racism and sexism. Prejudices have been set aside to fight the common enemy that threatens our lives every time we set foot out the door.

When this is all over, we must use our new state of mind to ensure that we never drift back to those dark days. The world can be a better place if we continue to work together.

A little housekeeping will be necessary first, though.

* * *

As someone who needs to laugh every day, I really look forward to the White House press briefings. But the last couple of days I have been really disappointed. Due to the medical advice given by Trump last week, his advisers have now banned him from answering any questions in public. They have realised that if allowed to speak again, he will definitely lose the next election.

Presidential hopeful Joe Biden currently believes himself to be a small pot plant called Brad and has been staying at home watering himself.

He has decided not to actively campaign for the job as he doesn't need to. He is quite happy to keep quiet while Trump keeps pressing his own self-destruct button.

People have already questioned Biden's mental agility as he keeps forgetting his name. But he is likely to be the next president anyway, mostly because he is not Trump. The choice for American voters will be a difficult one. Do you vote for a candidate obsessed with self-destruction, or one held up by strings? It's a difficult choice, but I think Pinocchio will win in November.

※ ※ ※

Boris is feeling better now. He will be returning to work tomorrow to take over from his assistant Dominic Cummings, who has really been running the country in his absence. Dominic Cummings has been seen sniffing around SAGE meetings of top scientists trying to work out a way of blaming coronavirus on Brussels.

Although most people in this country voted for Brexit (I think most have come to their senses though), public opinion is on the side of securing a deal with the EU. We have been warned by people who actually know about these things that leaving without a deal will be disastrous. Boris and Cummings have now worked out that they just may be able to get away with it. The British economy is going to collapse anyway, lorries won't be queuing up on motorways because there is no traffic, and as we have other things on our mind at the moment, nobody will notice. So expect to see a few news articles appearing on page four of the *Daily Telegraph* suggesting something along the lines of exit negotiations going badly as the Europeans won't agree to give us all the fish in the Bay of Biscay, or both sides of the Channel Tunnel, the Champagne region of France, Spain, and the best bits of Germany. So, as the

Europeans are being unreasonable, we are going to leave without a deal.

OTHER NEWS

Scientists have now found a way to communicate with coronavirus. They have been chatting with the flu virus for years and have finally been given an introduction to Covid-19.

In its first public statement, coronavirus has apologised for contaminating humans but insisted that it didn't mean it. It was quite happy living with the bats until someone ate one.

The representative of coronavirus is planning a press conference later to advise the American public on how to protect themselves from Trump. Coronavirus has also warned that after studying data, they are not yet convinced that Trump has reached his stupidity peak. They are advising that we can flatten the curve by taking away his Twitter account and denying all access to microphones.

Day 34

I THINK I WAS PATIENT ZERO

26th April 2020

My coffee machine broke down the other day, so as there is nobody left in my office, I went and got one to replace it. Got it home but it wouldn't work as the fuse had blown. I rummaged through the garage trying to find an old appliance to reuse the plug. Found an antique Teasmade with a plug. For anyone reading this below the age of sixty, this was a machine that replaced alarm clocks and woke you up in the morning by spraying scalding water over you. So, I didn't think I needed that any more. Tried to find a screwdriver, but after an hour of rummaging there was none to be found. I had heard that my local branch of the DIY store had reopened so went to buy one.

On arrival, I found the queue snaked around the car park twice and up the road, mixing with the supermarket queue next door. People were not sure which queue they were joining, but for me it didn't really matter as if I was in the wrong line, I could always buy a few beers and come back tomorrow.

Anyway, it was a nice day and I didn't have anything else to do so was happy to wait. When my turn came to enter, I noticed that the DIY store had changed considerably. Members of staff were walking around in spacesuits, and the checkout operators were dressed in bio-suits and sitting in Perspex bubbles. I thought this looked a little dangerous and they must know something I didn't, so decided the screwdriver was not that important and went next door for some essentials (mostly beer).

An interesting observation. Have you noticed that people avoid other people wearing masks? Alex, being smarter than most, chooses to wear a mask whenever we go to the shops or for our walk. I don't usually wear one as it makes my glasses steam up, but I respect her decision. On our daily walks, people tend to pass me keeping a nice two-metre distance, but when they see her coming, they either cross the road or turn around and run away. Can't really understand this, but decided not to go back to the DIY store for that screwdriver.

※ ※ ※

News emerged today that coronavirus has been in Europe since early January. Therefore, I think I've already had it.

We had to go to Istanbul (or for all the Greeks out there, Constantinople) via Luton Airport and Greece in late January. We had to spend three days there on business so decided to combine our trip with a little sightseeing. Alex's idea of "a little sightseeing" was to drop our bags at the hotel and drag me off to every museum, church and monument that she had ever heard of. After day two, I was exhausted and begging for mercy. The Blue Mosque, Hagia Sophia, the underground cisterns, royal palaces and the Grand Bazaar had all become a blur. My feet ached, together with the rest of my body.

By day three I had a fever, headache, and was coughing up broken glass. With no sympathy for my condition, and assuming that I only had a light dose of man flu, she continued to insist on allowing me to freeze my bits off on a romantic trip along the Bosphorus on an open boat filled with screaming kids, assorted Chinese people not wearing masks, and no beer in sight.

Feeling worse the next day, we left the hotel and went off to the airport to catch our flight home. The Turks, being very welcoming and hospitable people, don't want to see you leave, so make it really difficult. As we entered the terminal, our bags were scanned, luggage opened and checked. Passport inspected. We were then sent to passport control to be checked again. When my turn came, the police officer in the glass box was taking a lot of time looking at my passport. I was getting worried. He looked at me again, checked my visa and announced, "Big problem. Go to police desk."

Feeling poorly and even more worried now, I remembered *Midnight Express*. My mind wandered to that kilo bag of oregano in my suitcase from yesterday's visit to the spice market. The saffron looked a bit dodgy too. Was I an unwitting mule, duped into transporting mislabelled herbs that were going to be nicked from me by Mr Big when I arrived at Luton Airport?

It was all okay, though. My passport wouldn't scan but they let me go anyway.

Finally got home, went to bed, suffered for another week. So perhaps I was the super-spreader that nobody could find? It's not my fault, though. I promise that I didn't knowingly eat a bat. But the last kebab I had in central Istanbul tasted really funny.

Day 35

RECIPES FOR PIGEON

27th April 2020

Got up late today but thought I would make the effort. So, changed out of my night-time pyjamas and got dressed into my daytime pyjamas. It's raining and a bit dull out there, so not sure if the pigeon that visited the other day will come back. I have been leaving birdseed on the windowsill, hoping it will return. Can't light the barbecue in the rain, so if it does come back, I will have to make a casserole.

I have been busy studying recipes for pigeon since I first saw it and found quite a few ideas. The only problem that I can see at the moment is catching it. First, I must lure it within reach. Then what? Suddenly I remembered that we had bought a couple of pet rabbits for the grandchildren a year ago. They allowed me to keep them in a hutch in my garden, provided I promised not to eat them. I reluctantly agreed and took my responsibility quite seriously. I used to feed them bits of lettuce and clean out the hutch once a week. I even trained the dogs not to eat them, so they could roam around the garden nibbling on my AstroTurf. The biggest problem was catching them to put them back in the hutch. So, I went off to the local fishing shop and got a big landing net. Many happy hours passed with me running around the garden trying to net rabbits, and I got quite good at it.

The rabbits thought it was a game. They used to look forward every evening to being chased around the garden by an old red-faced fart waving a net, but I did get fit.

Eventually the grandchildren got bored and didn't want to visit them any more, rabbits being less interesting than PlayStations. So I was left with two rabbits that soon became one rabbit after the other was found with its legs in the air at the bottom of the hutch. The survivor was so lonely that I gave it away, hutch and all, to a friend who was grateful for a new pal for his guinea pig. But I kept the landing net.

But back to my plan. Went out to the garage. Found the net. Came back, spread some more birdseed on the windowsill, opened the window, sat behind the curtains keeping really quiet with landing net in hand, while congratulating myself on my plan to make a low-cost lunch. All it's cost me is birdseed from Amazon, and that was only tuppence a bag.

After six hours of waiting, the bird had not turned up. So, I looked around the curtains to see next door's cat sitting on the fence. He must have had the same idea, but not being as clever as me, he had not disguised himself as curtains and did not have a landing net. Not likely to catch my lunch with the cat sitting there, I went into the kitchen and made beans on toast.

Will try again tomorrow.

✳ ✳ ✳

As Dyson's ventilators are no longer needed by the NHS, I decided to get in the queue to get one cheap from eBay. Just being careful – you never know, they might run out. If I don't get the virus, I can always use it to hoover the stairs. I hope it has a plug on it, though, as I am not going back to the DIY shop for that screwdriver.

✳ ✳ ✳

As a lifelong Watford supporter, I am celebrating my team's new record. For those who don't know, Watford football team are quite a small club with only a few supporters, mostly Elton John and me. We are not used to success, so I'm happy to report that we haven't lost a match for almost two months, which is a new club record. Okay, they haven't actually been allowed to play any matches, but it's still a remarkable achievement. The goalkeeper is particularly happy because he has kept a clean sheet for ages.

When not wearing my club scarf as a mask, I am hanging it in my window to celebrate. Although I live near Luton, I haven't had a brick through my window yet. But I do live in hope. My barbecue needs an extension and I'm not going to risk going to the DIY store for more bricks.

Day 36

MY WIFE IS BECOMING A BIT TWITCHY

28th April 2020

As spring has arrived, Alex is becoming a bit twitchy and is starting to suggest that the house needs a freshen up. This usually involves an architect and scaffolding. My idea of freshening up the house is taking the bins out, but I don't think I am going to get away with that for long.

I am beginning to find pictures of living room designs and ornate mirrors being left (accidentally) near the beer fridge. Casual discussions are being guided towards my opinion of taking that wall out, and what do I think about a new conservatory? Normally I can get away with it by looking tired and commenting about my hard day at work. But that excuse won't work as she can see me wandering aimlessly around the house and spending my time doing nothing except hiding behind the curtains holding a net, trying to catch that pigeon.

A new plan is needed if I'm going to avoid months of scraping paint from under my fingernails and spending huge amounts of cash because the furniture no longer goes with the new paintwork and the kitchen drawers are getting a little wonky.

As a building surveyor, I do know a bit about building. Unfortunately, I was born with four thumbs and three elbows, so although I am really good at telling other people how to do it, I have trouble banging a nail into the wall. So, the thought of me getting involved in "a little DIY" usually means bringing in a builder on the second day to sort out the mess that I have made on the first day.

The last bit of DIY that I attempted was to fix a large LED TV on a hinged bracket in the bedroom. Purchased the TV and bracket. Got all my tools ready, spent a couple of hours trying to work out which way up the bracket goes. Drilled holes, screwed the bracket to the wall, connected the TV to the bracket.

Stood back to admire my work, and it all fell off the wall.

Luckily, the TV was only scratched and still worked, so tried again. This time I drilled different holes but deeper. Used longer screws to fix the bracket to the wall, fitted the TV to the bracket. Gave the TV a quick wobble to test it. Seemed fine so connected the wires, went off to find the remote control. As soon as my back was turned, I heard a loud noise as the whole thing fell off and hit the floor, breaking the TV and taking the wall plaster with it.

I was not confident Amazon would believe that the new TV recently purchased was damaged in transit, as it had screw holes in the back and was covered in wall plaster. So ordered another one.

While waiting for it to arrive, I tried to repair the wall and fit the bracket. Found some filler. Couldn't find a trowel so applied it with a dinner knife and a spoon. It didn't look great, but I thought it would be covered by the TV so no one would see it anyway. Waited for the filler to dry. Drilled the wall again. Screwed in the bracket, which promptly fell off again, taking the new filler with it together with more wall plaster.

Gave up and employed a builder.

This is all part of my wife's plan. She knows my track record with DIY. She also knows that I am a little bit arrogant and am likely to attempt intricate repairs and renovations myself. I'm a like a dog chasing a car, determined to catch it but no idea how to drive. So, she allows me to make all the preparations, cover furniture, paint the dogs instead of the walls. Spend a day wallpapering myself into a corner, and another day trying to get myself unstuck while generally causing chaos, before giving up and employing someone else to do it.

This time I will not fall into her trap. The builders are coming tomorrow to give me a quote.

Day 37
THE FOLLOWING INFORMATION COULD SAVE YOUR LIFE

29th April 2020

The following information could save your marriage, relationship, and even your life!
In these days of staying at home and

keeping ourselves and others safe, some relationships are beginning to strain.

I will use today's text to impart my long experience and wisdom learned to help others to avoid difficulties and keep their home a happy place.

HOW WOMEN THINK

The female of the species is cleverer than the male. They will sit down beside you, and out of nowhere comes a look that would melt glass. Eyes focused on you and burning a hole in your forehead.

Males have a problem recognising these signs and are gullible. We will usually shrug and carry on watching TV. Then heavy sighs start. We turn and ask, "Is there anything wrong?" This is always answered by "No, I'm fine".

At this point, do not believe her. This is a trap. If you stood up now and walked away, you would likely receive a vase over the head or a knife between your shoulder blades. You must persist.

"Are you sure you're okay?" you ask. Just being told that there is nothing wrong and believing her can be dangerous. Then the dreaded reply comes.

"Well, not really," she announces.

This is when you must be at your most careful. A lioness will always prowl around the savannah looking for herds of prey, but does not attack immediately. She will take her time hiding in the long grass, ears flattened against her head while studying the herd, looking for a weak or vulnerable animal that won't take too much catching and is unlikely to escape. Be warned: your wife has the same genes.

So you now suspect that she is not fine, but before you ask again you must think deeply about any recent indiscretions, or anything that you may have done, or not done, to upset her. At this point you must switch off the TV, set the Sky box to record what you were watching and start the examination.

Do not expect them to open up immediately. You must chip away at the shell slowly. Try suggesting that you will understand any problem and are happy to discuss her feelings. This should weed out the possibility that it's not you who is the victim of her anger. You might get lucky and it's someone else who has upset her.

Once you have either pacified her or you are lying bleeding on the floor, it's finished.

And once recovered, you can go back to watching the repeat of *Match of the Day*.

HOW MEN THINK

My wife sometimes asks what I am thinking. I usually answer "Nothing", and I'm being honest.

This is not a concept understood by females. Males have a superpower of being able to sit down and stare at the wall with absolutely no thoughts in their heads. Experience has taught me over the years that replying to this question in this way will only light the fire.

"You must be thinking of something?" She is beginning to get suspicious.

Quickly my brain reactivates as I search for a thought that I might get away with. I try the standard one: "I was just thinking how lovely you look today." Realising that she thinks that I have been caught thinking about the supermarket checkout operator with the low-cut dress while out buying beer, I'm now in trouble. In an attempt to defuse the situation, I try other explanations like "I had a hard day at work", "I'm worried about the mortgage", "I'm concerned about the influence of global warming on squirrels".

I'm in a dark tunnel and the only light I can see is from the oncoming train. There is no way out. So, she decides to pick away at my non-existent shell to get to the truth. Desperately, I fumble for a reason why I had a blank look on my face, but any reasons clutched at are not good enough and I must have a better one. After the standard grilling, and me promising to be good in future, I usually return to staring at the wall but with a good excuse ready in case I am interrogated again.

Men are simple creatures and generally honest. If asked if we have a problem, we usually answer truthfully.

Women are not simple. Their minds are like the contents of their handbags: full of irrelevant information all jumbled up in a pile so they can't find anything. They assume that we are the same. But we are not! We have simple needs, are mostly oblivious to our environment, easy to keep and quite happy with the small pleasures in life.

Men and women are different. If we accept *that*, we can be happy. But you need to be aware of the rules.

Day 38
DON'T READ THE INGREDIENTS

30th April 2020

MUSINGS FROM A PANDEMIC

Another day of lockdown. I have lost count of the days now, and I'm not sure if it's a weekend or a weekday.

I was thinking about making lunch and trying to invent new ways of cooking pasta. While rummaging through the cupboard for inspiration, I came across a tin of frankfurters. I never normally read ingredients on tins but as I have more time on my hands now, I made an exception. Top of the ingredient list is "mechanically reclaimed meat". What the hell is that? The picture on the tin looked good. Nice, tasty sausages nestling in a bun and coated in ketchup and mustard, with just enough onions to make my mouth water.

How do you mechanically reclaim meat – and reclaim from what? Could it be roadkill scraped up by a bulldozer? What was it before it was reclaimed? Yummy. That is going in my pasta dish today ...

Just off to the supermarket to stand in the queue for a few essentials (mostly beer and frankfurters).

❋ ❋ ❋

Recovering from a shock. Opened my beer fridge and it was empty. Someone has drunk it all. Looking around for someone else to blame, I was quite frustrated as Alex doesn't drink. The dogs had guilty looks on their faces, but it can't be them as they have trouble opening the bottles. I had to face the awful truth that it must have been me. I have recently suspected that I may have been slightly overindulging as the beer seems to be running out more frequently and my cheese puff supply has dwindled to just a few cases. As my dress code now only includes pyjamas and sweatpants, I have noticed that on the rare occasions I have to go to the office, all of my trousers have shrunk and I have to wear my shirt untucked as they won't zip up any more.

Drastic action must be taken. I have decided to extend my daily walk past the end of my garden. I have also decided to get fit and try a little home exercise. So, whipped off my sweatpants, nicked my wife's Zumba mat, and started with a little bending and stretching. Bent over, glanced back between my legs, and was horrified to see that I had grown another belly. Where my first belly used to be there was a little fold, and between that and my man bits *there was another one* bulging in between. I had no idea that you could get two bellies. What's all that about? I only need another four bellies and I can finally get that six-pack I've always wanted.

Depressed now, so going to sit in front of the TV and have a beer and a bag of cheese puffs to console myself.

※ ※ ※

The news is really boring at the moment. Trump is only allowed out to read from a script, so his wings have been clipped. Boris is telling us that the worst is over, but we must use a bit of common sense here. It's all very well saying that the roof is fixed when the sun is shining. Let's see when it rains again.

Trump has decided to tell us that the virus was manufactured in Wuhan, but somebody left the laboratory door open, so it jumped on a bus and found its way to the bat market. He is now threatening the Chinese that they are going to have to pay for the damaged caused.

He hasn't yet mentioned the 1918 Spanish flu pandemic that killed 50 million people as he has been informed that this world plague probably came from a chicken in Kansas. The Tin Man got really poorly, the Lion spent two weeks on a ventilator and the Scarecrow will never walk again. Dorothy got blamed for spreading it to Munchkinland and the Yellow Brick Road had to be sterilised.

Trump is thinking about blaming this on the Wicked Witch of the West, but may change his mind if he can pin it on someone in New York who votes for the Democrats.

Day 39

HOW DARE THEY LET ME IN!

1st May 2020

B it depressed today. I woke up early so decided to pop down to my local supermarket to beat the queue. I did need a few essentials (mostly beer). Arrived at the car park and found it to be unusually quiet. No queues snaking around the side of the store, no jams of people standing on their bit of red tape waiting to be let in.

Feeling quite pleased with myself, I locked the car and followed the arrows marked on the pavement to take me up the road past the riot barriers that funnel you to the entrance. I pushed my trolley into the lobby, past the security guard, and started my shopping.

I was heading towards the beer aisle when I noticed that the few shoppers around were quite old and looked a little infirm. Focused on the selection of beer, I nearly missed the big sign informing me that "This supermarket is currently open for elderly and vulnerable customers only". In my haste to beat the rush, I had inadvertently strayed into the store at the wrong time and *they let me in*!

I went back to the security guard. I apologised and asked if it was correct that the supermarket was only open for old people?

He nodded his head and confirmed. "But I shouldn't be here now," I protested. He looked at me, assuming I was a little strange, and reconfirmed that I was fine to be in here at this time. I was getting desperate now.

"Aren't you going to throw me out?" I

asked hopefully. He turned his back and wandered off.

This was really depressing. I know I got up early, didn't comb my hair and probably still had my just-got-up face, but that was no excuse. How dare they not throw me out?

So went home. Found some of my wife's hair dye, touched up the grey bits. Combed my hair, put on a clean shirt, and went off to see if I could get thrown out of Sainsbury's.

The government has announced today that they exceeded their promised coronavirus testing rate of over 100,000 tests by the end of April. The actual number of tests carried out was 73,191. The rest are in the post. The government has also confirmed that the NHS have all the PPE necessary – although most of it is still stuck on the runway at Istanbul airport, they have included this in their calculations as it's in the post.

In these days of lockdown, we need to laugh every day. Laughter has been proved to increase your resistance to disease and make you feel generally better. White blood cell production is increased, giving us a better chance of staying well. So why have they locked Trump away? The world needs entertainment. We need to stay well. Please let him out for at least an hour a day. The world would be a happier, healthier place.

Day 40

I LIKE IT WITH EXTRA HAIR AND NIPPLES

2nd May 2020

Everything around me seems to be breaking. As yesterday was a nice day, I decided to light the barbecue. My barbecue is a bit rickety but functional. The great thing about this device is that it has a big electrical spit-roast mechanism that can turn and cook anything up to a whole lamb. An even better thing about this device is that it doesn't take any work apart from occasionally feeding it with lumps of charcoal, so it's been my long-term excuse for doing absolutely nothing for hours while the barbecue does all the work. But I must be there to watch it go around while sitting in my comfy garden chair, feet up, and drinking (mostly beer). Alex knows that she can't ask me to do anything while "cooking" as I can't leave the barbecue in case the food burns.

Yesterday I got a whole pork belly, just the way I like it: with extra hair and nipples. Tied it onto the spit, sprinkled it with a little salt and oregano. Set the motor and sat back to watch it for a few hours. I was just getting comfortable when the motor started making grinding noises and fell off. This was a disaster. I wasn't too worried about the meat; it was the sudden loss of my excuse for doing nothing that distressed me. I had to think fast.

I took the partly cooked pork off the spit. Wrapped it in foil and went into the kitchen to pop it in the oven. The oven didn't work, so checked the fuse board. That had tripped when the barbecue fell to pieces. So reset the fuses, got the oven working, and carried on looking for something to make me look busy but without too much effort.

I decided to make some bread. I weighed some flour, found an old packet of yeast, added it to the bread maker, dragged my comfy chair in from the garden, and sat between the oven and bread maker with beer in hand.

A little later I was awoken by the smoke alarm screaming and dogs howling. My pork was ready. Took it out of the oven. It was a little well done but I could always scrape the black bits off. Opened the bread maker and found a flat brown disc at the bottom of the container. Not only did my barbecue die, but the yeast committed suicide, the smoke alarm stopped working, and I now need an electrician to replace my fuse box.

Going out to visit the DIY store to get some barbecue repair bits. If I join the wrong queue, I can always buy more beer instead to drown my sorrows.

IN OTHER NEWS

A new cure for coronavirus is sweeping social media sites. People are drinking their own urine. In all fairness, although disgusting, it is not as bad for you as injecting bleach.

They believe knocking back your own urine will not only cure all manner of health issues but will also give you more energy. The home page of the 4,981-member group Urine Therapy says: "Does it work? Better than you could ever imagine!"

Drinkers are advised: "The midstream of the first morning urine is the most important drink of the day."

Trump will be adding this to his growing list of recommendations during his White House briefing later – if they let him out.

Day 41
I THOUGHT I WOULD START WITH COOKING SOMETHING SMALL

3rd May 2020

Good news!! Barbecue fixed.

Sat in the garden yesterday with my rickety old barbecue in pieces, refitted the motor, tested it, and it works. Going to give it a test run later. Comfy chair dragged out of the kitchen and positioned in front of the barbecue. Footstool ready, table beside the chair for my beer, and Alexa plugged in (might need someone to argue with later). Ready to cook. I did miss it – watching the paddle go around in the bread maker is just not the same.

I thought I would start by cooking something small and build up to larger animals slowly. So, I sent a message to my daughter enquiring as to the health of the grandchildren's guinea pigs, but she hasn't returned my call yet. She does spoil those kids.

Now looking forward to a busy afternoon cooking and doing absolutely nothing. Perfect.

It looks like the government is making plans to end the lockdown. Manufacturers of traffic cones have already returned to work, ready for the traffic to return to normal so they can go back to causing chaos. Temporary traffic lights are being put in place, ready to be switched on as soon as holes start being dug in the roads for no reason other than to move dirt from one hole to another.

Police and sniffer dogs are getting ready to visit relaxed-looking wives and husbands who are claiming that their partners have been socially isolating somewhere else. Usually under newly planted rose bushes at the bottom of the garden.

Toilet roll manufacturers are bracing themselves for a drop in orders as it's going to take at least two years for us to use up our stockpiled supplies in our garages and sheds.

Councillors are being trained to deal with weaning us off our new-found hobby of drinking ourselves to death. The new Nightingale Hospital in the ExCel Centre will start to move out the beds and replace them with circles of chairs ready for when Alcoholic Anonymous move in to take over the building.

When I finally suspend my retirement and go back to work, I think I have to change a few things. I haven't worn a suit and tie for over a month, my trousers have all shrunk, I can't see where I'm going as my hair is too long. Been sitting looking out of the window for so long that my brain has started to melt and I've recently started dribbling

PETER BARBER

Please, please, Boris, can we have just one more month? Please?

Day 42

A FUNNY THING ABOUT BANANAS

4th May 2020

Good news. Walmart in America will no longer be selling guns to children. The age restriction has now been raised to twenty-one. However, in Maine, Alaska, Minnesota or New York State you can sell a rifle to someone over sixteen. In Minnesota, as long as it's not in the city, you can sell a rifle to a fourteen-year-old without parental consent.

The recent panic buying of guns has surprised and delighted retailers, who have not questioned their good fortune and have not told their customers that coronavirus is very, very small and unlikely to be seen through a telescopic sight attached to an automatic assault rifle. Undeterred, these people are buying huge quantities of these guns and bullets in the hope of protecting themselves against this growing menace.

But. Hope is on the horizon. These guns may be of use after all. The latest plague to visit is going to be a nasty creature known as the "murder hornet".

Apparently, these beasties can almost kill you by looking at you. These being up to two inches long, the gun-toting rednecks are polishing their weapons and stocking up on bullets as they will now have something to aim at.

In this country, Walmart do not sell high-powered assault rifles, so we will have to settle for a can of fly spray and a roll of newspaper.

Government policy has always advised that measures to deal with coronavirus will be dictated by the science and only when the time is right. This is nothing to do with the state of the run-down health service, years of cuts and austerity resulting in a complete lack of PPE other than rubber gloves to take the bins out.

After dithering about for the past 12 weeks telling us that wearing masks makes no difference and probably won't protect us against the virus, they have checked Amazon and found that they are now available. So suddenly the science dictates that wearing a mask *will* protect us. We are not allowed to wear the ones that actually work, though, as these have to be reserved for the NHS. We will have to make do with the ones from the DIY store that are usually worn when sanding down the door frame.

I am thinking of popping out for a few essentials. I read yesterday about Brazilian wandering spiders being found in a bunch of bananas brought from Tesco's. This South American spider's venom is the deadliest in the world, and its bite can also cause an erection lasting up to four hours.

I usually get my essential supplies from Morrison's. But today I'm off to Tesco's for my shopping. Forget mostly beer, I'm going for other essentials (mostly bananas).

Day 43

A FROWN CREEPS ACROSS MY FACE AS MY BRAIN CELLS KICK IN

5th May 2020

Every morning I sit down to write my daily post. I usually have absolutely no idea of what to include until I start. Then either a grin or a frown creeps across my face as my brain cells kick in. Today is a little of both.

Just saw on the news that the PPE sourced

from Turkey is in a warehouse gathering dust. It is claimed that when the full amount finally reached the UK, inspectors from the Health and Safety Executive found it did not conform to UK standards.

The Turks have assured the British government that the delivery was exactly as ordered. The lacy aprons were of the best quality, and the flower pattern was nicely printed. The surgical gloves normally used by vets to extract little cows from big cows were of the best quality available, and the masks provided were anti-mist with extra-long snorkels.

Government officials have been advised not to order any more essential supplies using Alexa.

Yesterday's newspapers had their priorities a little confused. The main story was about government adviser Neil Ferguson, who resigned as he was caught breaking lockdown rules by indulging in illicit rumpy-pumpy. If illicit nookie is a reason for resignation, most of the cabinet ministers, including Boris, should be reconsidering their positions.

The main story should have been the fact

that we are now the worst affected country in Europe and have recorded the most deaths. So far, official government statistics show around 30,000, but some sources put this as high as 50,000. The government is disputing that we are the worst affected in Europe and has stated that other countries have a different way of counting. I thought most people, regardless of nationality, usually start with 1-2-3 and then continue.

Boris has never been particularly good at figures. This is proved by a big red bus wheeled out during the Brexit campaign.

Government policy has now changed the way that new rules are announced. The new system involves the scheduling of an announcement from the prime minister for a week's time, meanwhile leaking it to the press and keeping their heads down to see who bites. Any public uproar can then be denied and put down to newspaper speculation, and the government can claim that they weren't going to say that anyway.

This seems to have worked before, so why change a good thing?

Boris Johnson is beginning to come under pressure from non-tame newspapers who are suggesting that he has mishandled the coronavirus pandemic. In late January, Boris was busy trying to raise money for the "Big Ben Bong" and a party in Trafalgar Square to celebrate Brexit. Meanwhile, Germany had already started closing factories and testing its population.

Okay. Had my rant of the day. Tomorrow back to normal. We might get lucky and the pubs open. My local pub windows have lost all their flavour now and my tongue has dried out.

Now sitting in my garden. Enjoying the sunshine and dreaming of the good things in life (mostly beer) while waiting for my Tesco bananas to hatch.

Day 44

I NOW HAVE BIGGER BOOBS THAN MY WIFE

6th May 2020

This is worrying ... New evidence has come to light that obesity increases your risk of developing worse symptoms if you catch coronavirus. I have begun to realise that I'm not as slim as I used to be. I think the enforced lockdown is having an effect, so not my fault.

In the last few days, I have become more and more distressed as I discover even more bellies. Looking in the mirror, I have noticed that my top front belly seems to have spread to either side of my hips and is now bulging over the side of my sweatpants. My lower front belly is getting bigger, completely covering my man bits which I haven't seen for a month. And I've just found another one under my chin that wobbles when I talk. I haven't checked my arse yet as I can't reach it, but suspicious there may be another one lurking behind me somewhere. If so, my lifelong ambition of a six-pack will have been realised. Not quite how I imagined it, though.

I now have bigger boobs than my wife. My belly button has transformed into a funnel, which I only noticed when I inadvertently started to leave peanut shells in there while watching TV. My extra-large T-shirt is now stopping short of what used to be my waist, revealing a line separating my upper belly from the lower one. My bath needs less water, but the shower needs more. I can only touch my toes with a stick, and the only exercise I get nowadays is chewing.

When I gave up smoking, I put on weight but managed to get away with it by using some of the old excuses.

These included "big bones". Not going to get away with that.

"It's glandular." Yeah, I have a gland that makes me lazy and spend too much time stuffing my face and drinking beer.

Or how about: "That is not fat, it's rippling muscle"? Problem is that my muscles keep on rippling for ten minutes after I sit down.

A new excuse is needed. So, I checked Google. Came up with the following quiz, which I completed.

1. You wake up one morning with breasts a full cup size larger. *Tick.*
2. You are E-X-H-A-U-S-T-E-D. *Tick. There is a lot of effort required to chew.*
3. You're drooling. *Tick. Usually when daydreaming about the good things in life (mostly beer).*
4. Your short-term memory is completely shot. *Tick. Sometimes I even forget where I put the beer.*

5. You're always hungry. *Tick. Constantly munching cheesy puffs and still hungry.*
6. You eat unusual food. *Tick. Been trying to get hold of guinea pig for weeks but had to settle for barbecued squirrel.*
7. You can't walk up a set of six steps without getting winded. *Tick. All my energy has been used up with chewing and opening beer.*
8. You cry at the drop of a hat. *Tick. But only when I run out of beer.*
9. You've never drunk so much. *Tick. (Mostly beer.)*

So, got to the end of the quiz, pressed the result button.

Got a message:

"CONGRATULATIONS. YOU ARE PREGNANT."

I know there are many of you out there with the same problem. So now you don't need to feel too bad. There's always a good excuse somewhere – you just need to look for it.

Day 45

HAY FEVER SEASON IS HERE

7th May 2020

Alex and I were sitting in the garden enjoying the sunshine when the sound of a sneeze was heard over the fence. Alex ran into the house, put her mask on, grabbed the industrial-sized acid-and-Dettol spray can, poked it over the fence and started to squirt the neighbour's garden with the neighbour still sitting in it.

I was in the supermarket earlier getting my essentials (mostly beer) when some poor soul sneezed. The whole aisle froze; people turned and looked for the disease-ridden virus-carrying individual who had the bad grace to let out a sneeze in their space.

People's expressions have changed. In the old days we didn't even think about sneezing; it was natural, like yawning. The world is now full of ugly-looking hay fever sufferers who have red faces and bulging eyes from trying to stifle their sneezes while out shopping. It is impossible to stifle a sneeze without looking ugly as blowbacks are common and can cause real damage. But not as much damage as being chased out of a supermarket by an angry mob armed with frozen lamb legs and baguettes. In the pre-virus days, the correct form was to say "Bless you". Now the expression is more likely to be "Fuck you". This is usually screamed over their shoulders while running away and spraying themselves with hand sanitiser.

Boris is due to speak to us from Downing Street tomorrow. Government policy has been filtered through the tame media who have been publishing ideas all week to gauge public opinion. Boris has been hiding behind his desk with his tin hat on, waiting for the screams of protest. But he now has a fair idea of what he can get away with. So far, he seems to have settled on opening garden centres as we may need to grow our own food if this continues any longer. And there is a shortage of shovels in supermarkets, having been used to assist husbands and wives who currently have their nearest and dearest self-isolating in the freezer, so they can dig a hole and isolate them somewhere else. The freezer will be needed for the vegetables now.

Schools may be reopening. This is a great idea. Government scientists have claimed children are unlikely to get coronavirus, but even Domestos wouldn't deal with the 99 per cent of germs these little super-spreaders bring home. It's like my mother's driving record. She's been on the road for forty years and never had an accident. But she's seen thousands (usually in her rear-view mirror). Other drivers in the village have a Facebook group to report what time she goes out so they can stay home.

※ ※ ※

The news this morning revealed that the government has decided to enforce quarantine on all passengers arriving at airports from abroad. This particular horse bolted at the beginning of March, closed the stable door behind it and turned the lights off, and moved into a bigger barn and had little horses. But the government has always insisted they will be led by the science and take appropriate action at the right time.

Official Home Office figures have shown that that just 273 people arriving at UK airports were asked to quarantine in the last four months, while the total number of arrivals was 18.1 million. So now that nobody is flying anywhere, the government, led by the science, has now considered it to be "the right time". Brilliant.

As the airlines are beginning to dust off their planes and start selling tickets, I was thinking about going back to Greece. I need a change and could go there to do nothing somewhere else, as getting bored doing nothing here.

However, as Greece have had a similar arrangement since early April, we would have to quarantine at Athens airport for two weeks before being let out just in time to catch the flight back to England. Then another fourteen days' quarantine at Heathrow. I'll send you a postcard.

Day 46

MY LITTLE DOG IS A BIT DIFFERENT

8th May 2020

So ... how are your teeth? Are you brushing and flossing properly? Are you up to date on your check-ups with the dentist and hygienist?

If not, you are in trouble. As most dentists have closed because of the coronavirus pandemic and were having trouble finding your teeth through your mask, we have to resort to home remedies. Pliers have sold out on Amazon, and Black & Decker are cashing in on new attachments for their masonry drills.

Pharmacies are now selling out of DIY filling kits and nail files. We are getting so good at home dentistry that I think this will be a trend in the future.

We are now going back to the old cures. Tasting wee will tell you if you have diabetes. Some people are adding ice and lemon for a new type of refreshment.

Leeches are becoming fashionable again. I thought I'd try a couple to lose a bit of weight. But when it came time to remove the little buggers, I thought my belly button was one and now have second-degree burns on my navel. Still can't find the leeches. I think they're hiding in my bum crack and are safely out of reach.

Two bricks are the new vasectomy kit. As long as you protect your thumbs it should be okay, but it does make your eyes water.

As people are now avoiding hospitals, casualty departments are so empty that the NHS has started advertising. They are assuring us that they are still open so if you are having a stroke or a heart attack, it probably won't go away on its own. Cuts and grazes are still being treated. Even people who have injected or drunk bleach are welcome. But if you have toothache, please stay away.

※ ※ ※

As the only permitted purpose for leaving home is a quick dog walk or the supermarket, I took my dogs out this morning. I have noticed that all dogs are now posh breeds. Scruffy mongrels are a thing of the past as people are going for expensive makes, like choosing their handbags and shoes. My little dog is a bit different. We found her near our house on the Greek island of Evia. She was a tiny puppy with a broken leg. She was sitting in the garden looking sorry for herself, so we adopted her. She is a strange-looking character. Her long snout is from a whippet, her body a little rotund like a bulldog; plus she has the short, skinny legs of a dragonfly and the tail of a rat.

We wrapped her up in a blanket and went off to find a vet who could fix her leg. We soon discovered that there are no vets on the island. My wife being Greek and more inventive than me decided to find an alternative. After a few phone calls to local medical professionals and being told loudly that "We are doctors, madam, and don't treat animals", my wife screaming back at them, she finally found an orthopaedic surgeon who agreed to take a look. We arrived at his consulting room above a cake shop and sat down among the other waiting patients, until eventually the doctor came out, took a quick look, and sent my wife to the pharmacy for some plaster and bandages. He couldn't reset the leg but patched her up and recommended a vet in Athens. Finally, leg repaired, new plaster applied, she was on the way to recovery.

 The next problem was to get her home. Not being able to find an airline that would take us, I decided on another way. So left the dog in the care of a friend. Took a flight back to Luton. Went home, picked up the car and spent five days driving back to Greece via the Channel Tunnel, through France, Switzerland and Italy, then two days on the ferry. Got the dog in the car, pet passport sorted, and drove back to England with dog happily snoozing on the back seat. In all a 4,000-mile round trip and about £6,000 with the vet bills.

Sometimes other dog owners look down their noses at mine and ask: "What breed of dog is that?" I usually reply, "No idea, but it cost more than yours."

Day 47
SORRY? RUN THAT PAST ME AGAIN ...

9th May 2020

Last night Boris broadcast his long-awaited announcement on the stages to lift the lockdown. I found it a bit confusing, together with the other 67 million people of the UK. Apparently, we are now allowed to go for more walks but can only meet one person from another household, staying two metres apart. But only in a field or park, not in your garden or anywhere else. We can go back to work. But not on a bus or a train, and only if you work on a construction site ... But Boris, we have always been allowed to do that as sites are still open.

You can play golf. But only with yourself as you are not permitted to meet anyone else. Garden centres are opening, though.

After more than a week of press speculation and a garbled briefing, the only thing that has changed is that we can buy a plant – but not today. Maybe Wednesday?

Passengers arriving from abroad are going to be required to quarantine for 14 days. That will put the final nail in the travel industry coffin. This has nothing to do with coronavirus but more to do with the government's determination to keep everyone out after the Brexit negotiations fail. If they had any intention of keeping the airlines in business, they would have done this a different way. But that would involve common sense. It would be straightforward to give everyone arriving a quick nose swab, then text them the result in a couple of days. Thereby keeping the airlines running and reaching the testing target quicker. Then, perhaps we can go on holiday. But am I oversimplifying?

I had to drive into London today to visit a site. It's dangerous out there! People have forgotten how to drive. My theory is: due to the cold weather, cyclists are taking their cars out and driving them like they ride their bikes.

Drivers wearing Lycra and cycle helmets are peering through windscreens, running traffic lights, over and undertaking while weaving around cars and lorries, and generally trying to kill themselves and others. When the rest of their pals get back on their real bikes there will be chaos.

Day 48
NOT ONLY IS IT REALLY HARD TO WATCH ...

10th May 2020

So, Boris has now clarified Sunday's announcement.
	After the confusing public address

given on Sunday with the aid of graphs and tables, he has now changed his slogan from "Stay at Home" to "Be Alert". That helps!

I did try to watch his question-and-answer session in parliament yesterday but ended up even more confused than before. So that we can all get a grip on the government proposals, we should start by asking Boris politely to try ending a sentence before he begins another one and then goes back to the second part of the sentence that he started ten sentences ago, while uttering "err" between each word. Not only is it really hard to watch, but he gives the impression that he still has no clue what he is advising us to do.

But. Good news. After reading the new fifty-page revised government guideline document, you can now go out to buy a plant, and you can walk there if you want.

Yes, we do need to go back to work. Otherwise, the economy will completely collapse. But this must be weighed against the potential loss of life and severe illness if we get it wrong. As a boss of my own company, it does not make sense to bring people back off furlough if the phones aren't ringing and there is nothing to do. So, we do need to be looking at a gradual recovery rather than rushing into the possibility of going through this again. I started my business from nothing, so I am sure that I can do it again when all this is over. But we must be patient.

Taking government advice, I went to work today. Watered the plants, brushed the cobwebs away, checked for emails. None there. Checked the answerphone. Nobody called. Sat at my desk. Stared out of the window. I think I saw a pigeon. I'm here, still doing nothing, but at work doing it.

As an old fart, I have picked up a few things during my long existence on this planet. I know that people are suffering. Normal life has changed into something unrecognisable. But experience has taught me that no matter how dark things look, just wait and see.

In future you will be able to look back on this part of your life and be grateful for the experience and see it with different eyes. So much good will come out of it, but you haven't even begun to realise it yet. You can always reread these posts to remind you.

Going to close the office and go home now. I heard that my daughter's been tempting squirrels with cheesy Wotsits, so going to fire up the barbecue. Who knows, I might get lucky.

Day 49

MY WIFE HAS A THING ABOUT WASHING STUFF

11th May 2020

I went to work today as I had a couple of appointments. Things seem to be waking up a little. On my way home I passed by the supermarket for some essentials. I parked the car, grabbed a trolley and ran towards the door. An attendant stopped me and pointed out that there was a queue. I looked around and saw the snake of people queuing around the corner which I'd missed in my haste to grab some beers before going home. I was delighted. The attendant had obviously realised that I was neither elderly nor infirm, so wasn't allowed in and had to queue.

Then he added, "If you can't walk properly, though, I can let you in." I was devastated. I thought I was walking normally, no limp. I wasn't dragging my feet, no wheelchair, so how dare he offer to let me in ahead of the line? I assured him that I was quite healthy and happy to join the queue. "If you're sure, grandad," he replied. I'm not going there again.

On my way from the supermarket, I passed by the gym. Part of the new government easing of lockdown is to allow fitness centres to re-open. I have joined many gymnasiums over recent years. Never actually gone to work out, but at least I had good intentions.

This time, I was determined to adopt a new fitness regime and start to exercise and lose some of my new-found bellies. I sometimes have this overwhelming desire to get fit. I have visions of myself on rowing machines, jogging happily on the rolling road, and lifting weights to build up my muscles so I don't need to hide my several bellies with dark-coloured loose-fitting garments. I could dig out my old Speedos from the bottom of my underwear drawer and practise kicking sand in people's faces next time I go on holiday.

But before that happens, I need to put the work in. So, I looked online, selected a health club with a nice bar and restaurant attached, took a look at the pool and jacuzzi. Didn't take too much notice of the actual exercise area. I can build up to that later. Signed up, and ready to go.

The last time I joined a fitness centre, I signed a one-year contract, set up monthly payments, and found that I didn't really have the time to visit.

After six months I started to feel a little guilty, so got my swimming costume, towel and shower gel, and used my entrance card for the first time. I walked through the gymnasium, out the other side, past the pool, got changed and got into the jacuzzi. After an hour of congratulating myself for joining a gym (at least I turned up), I went back to the changing rooms, had a shower, walked out of the shower across the tiled floor, trod on some soap. Suddenly, my legs were where my head used to be and I crashed to the floor, breaking my elbow. I didn't go again. This time is different. Perhaps ...

※ ※ ※

The reason I'm late today is that my Alex has a thing about washing stuff. She has always been very house-proud and spends most of her time cleaning, polishing and rearranging furniture, to the extent that I sometimes wonder if I have entered the wrong house and have to go back outside and check the number.

Since the coronavirus pandemic, she has been fixated on washing everything that I even look at. My beer cans are all sticky from sanitiser gel, the floors are always slippery, and the dogs are permanently wet and smell of bleach. She took to washing my keys last week and I found that I couldn't get into my office as they had gone rusty. Twice a week, she goes to her dad's to cook, clean and generally make sure he's okay. Today she arrived and started his meal, and while she was waiting, put her car keys into a bowl of bleach and water to sterilise them. When she left she was surprised to find that when trying to start her car, the alarm went off and the lights flashed. She had no idea there was a battery in the key which was needed to start the car, and she had melted it.

Finally home now. So for the first time for months, I've had a busy day. Going to have a day off tomorrow to recover.

Day 50
I TOLD YOU I WAS ILL

12th May 2020

Thankfully, Covid seems to be on the decline.
    But beware. There is a new virus sweeping Europe. This sneaky new infection

brushes past our wives, leaving a few sniffles before departing and heading our way.

It selectively attacks men, but it waits until wives and girlfriends have caught a quick dose and brushed it off as a slight chill. But by the time it gets to us, it has transformed into a virulent and terrifying affliction akin to swamp fever.

This devious virus is using our wives against us. We begin to feel poorly. We look for a little sympathy. But they have already passed the much milder form and want to know what all the fuss is about.

We lay in our beds with sweat running into fevered eyes, begging our other halves to show us a little sympathy. "A tea would be nice, and perhaps an aspirin?" we ask. "How about breakfast in bed today?" we plead.

But it falls on deaf ears.

We are suffering from the dreaded man flu.

This terrible pathogen has evaded medical science and has become feared by men all over the globe. Our partners have no idea how serious it can be. Whereas she only had a mild sniffle, by the time it infected us it had grown into a serious and debilitating disease. This requires an abundance of sympathy, lots of sandwiches, hot soup, a few grapes nicely peeled, and a freshly poured beer or two while huddled on the sofa watching TV.

But do they listen? Of course not.

So, we have to fight this alone and get our own beer, while being assured we are babies and making a fuss.

Spike Milligan's epitaph on his gravestone includes the phrase "Dúirt mé leat go raibh mé breoite", Irish for "I told you I was ill".

So, ladies. Have some sympathy for your suffering husbands this year. Man flu is not to be taken lightly.

The government has now announced that they have at last found an antibody test kit that works. This should be able to tell us if we had the virus. Our recent bout of coughing with a high fever and spending five days trying to breathe was a clue, but now it can be official. These tests are likely to prove that 99 per cent of the population have already had coronavirus, but wives ignored the illness as usual, and men were not taken seriously as it was likely to be a dose of man flu – and they know how we exaggerate that one. So the 16 million spent on the last test kits has not been wasted and has been sent to the House of Commons bar to be used as swizzle sticks to mix the gin and tonic. A separate order of defective paper umbrellas is also on the way from Turkey.

* * *

Trump is now in panic mode. He has finally worked out that unless he can pull something out of the White House hat quickly, he is doomed to lose the election. He is currently spending his time furiously trying to find someone else to take the rap, but there are so many cock-ups he will need a lot of stooges.

The normal way to bring yourself back to favour politically would be to start a war. However, most of the perceived enemies have been rather quiet lately, not wishing to provoke him, as they know he's on the way out and it's just a matter of time before he shoots his own foot off, which will probably be in his mouth at the time. The race card won't work at the moment as people have lost interest in Mexicans, Muslims and anyone who isn't white American, as they have other things to worry about. The "tremendous" wall that the Mexicans were going to pay for is still on the drawing board, and the Mexicans don't want to come anyway as they don't want to catch coronavirus.

Trump's devious little mind has worked

out that if he stays clinging to the White House, he is fairly safe. However, the day he loses the election, his political enemies, together with the long-abused press of America, will delve into every shady deal, every corner of his life to forensically examine every move he has made in the past fifty years. If he had any idea of a nice retirement playing golf and relaxing in one of his luxurious hotels, he needs to think again. The old expression that you should be nice to people on the way up, as you will certainly meet them again on the way down, is a saying that he has obviously never heard of.

So, in the short term he will continue spitting poison at journalists, will try to discredit any politician that isn't him, and continue his rampage until the American voter decides that's enough.

Anyway. Enough of that!

Day 51

A WAR ON FAT PEOPLE

13th May 2020

Sex workers are now demanding to be allowed to furlough like the rest of us. They don't consider it to be fair that we are all laying on our backs and getting paid for it.

They are demanding to be allowed not to lay on their backs and still be paid.

Boris is about to wage a war on fat people. He is convinced that the reason he had severe symptoms during his recent coronavirus infection is because he is overweight. Now that he's encouraged us all to stay at home for the past two months and do nothing but eat and drink, most of the population will need to watch out for whatever he is planning for us to ensure weight loss. He probably won't need to do anything as the worst recession the world has ever known is on the way, so we are likely to lose weight anyway thanks to living on a diet of shoes and grass – we won't be able to afford real food.

Undeterred, he is still banging on about using our bikes instead of driving or using public transport. London is dangerous enough already with hordes of cyclists buzzing around my car like angry bees while I'm trying to drive in a straight line and not run them over. Boris has already spent millions on dedicated cycle superhighways and lanes, but, not happy with that, they want my bit of road too.

Next, the outside lane of the M1 and M25 will be converted into a cycle lane. This will be full of middle-aged old farts like me, furiously pedalling to work with our briefcase in the front basket. I suppose I would get fit, but I would have to leave home one hour before I got home yesterday to make sure I'm not late tomorrow.

Went to work today. Didn't do much, mostly nothing except look out the window. I thought I saw that pigeon again. Might bring some birdseed on Monday – never know, I might be able to catch that one. I hear that the weather is going to be good soon, so should get the barbecue lit.

The good news is that it's Friday. Looking forward to the weekend, putting my feet up and doing nothing ... again.

Day 52

IT'S THE EUROVISION SONG CONTEST TIME

14th May 2020

As the Eurovision Song Contest is cancelled this year, Great Britain is celebrating that its entry didn't come its usual last. According to Spotify, we would have come in at a respectable fourteenth place, behind the Austrian bearded lady singing about a bird. RESULT!!!

I really do look forward to this contest every year. It is an eye-opening showcase of European talent.

Previous winners include:

Dana International, who was the first transgender person to win the competition. I had no idea she was a he until I read the newspapers the next morning.

The Portuguese entry, who sang in a girl's voice while trying to catch butterflies, his sister lurking behind and stroking him in a weird way.

Ukraine presented drag queen Verka Serduchka, who dressed in tinfoil with a windmill on his head. They didn't win in 2007, but did manage second place. Ruslana went one better when she shocked and delighted the men of Europe with her 2004 entry, "Wild Dances", performed while not wearing any knickers.

MUSINGS FROM A PANDEMIC

The entry that didn't win, but should have, was the Polish entry about milkmaids announcing that they were Slavic. Nobody took any notice of the song, but 20 million Europeans were sitting on the edge of their seats, waiting for their boobs to finally fall out.

The normal razzmatazz is being replaced by a virtual pre-recorded show which will feature the best of Europe's performers.

As usual, there was controversy during the performances. The Romanian singing vampire was disqualified after biting the Moldavian fairy wearing a pointy hat and riding a unicycle.

The singing turkey from Ireland was plucked and stuffed and put in the oven even before he finished his song – an easy mistake as he was already wrapped in tinfoil.

The Russian entry, a grandma tap-dancing while knitting, didn't go too well as halfway through the performance she dropped a stitch and was deported to a gulag in Siberia.

The women wearing voluminous sequinned evening dresses were complaining that the special effects were overdone as the dry ice was getting under their skirts and they were getting frostbite on their testicles. The clown playing a barrel organ was disqualified after the handle fell off, and Finland's entry of a band of monsters playing loud music badly were thrown off stage for eating the tap-dancing horse, so the Albanians couldn't get home.

But the voting was true to form and, as always, fair. Cyprus and Greece gave each other 12 points even though none of their singers turned up.

Sweden, Norway and Finland made their usual deal and are currently in joint second place.

Australia did quite well as Germany and Switzerland thought it was a misprint and that they were voting for Austria.

The overall winner was announced when someone dropped a cigarette on the studio cat, who then ran into a box of fireworks. The judges said it was the best voice of the evening and the special effects were amazing.

So watch the show on BBC1 tonight. I will report again tomorrow when the confirmed results are in.

Day 53

I'M FAT

15th May 2020

It looks like the lockdown will soon be ending. It's time to purge myself of my unhealthy habits and get fit.

So, I rummaged through the bedroom drawers, found my old tracksuit, located my trainers and got dressed, determined to start the fitness regime today. Went to tie my trainers but couldn't reach them, so changed those for slip-on pumps. I woke up my overweight, unfit dogs and told them my intention. They both had a blank look seeing me dressed funny, but the penny dropped when I showed them their leads. After a few moments of them excitedly bouncing around eager to go, I plugged my iPod into my ears, set my Log My Run distance calculator app, and off we went.

The dogs' enthusiasm lasted until the first corner. After that they started to flag and I took over, dragging them instead. By the time we arrived at the park, they were wandering aimlessly around, sniffing the odd grass patch and fencepost, but then I led them through the park towards the open fields. With me walking at super pace, and them taking ten minutes per sniff, we weren't getting very far.

It was my intention to power-walk through the cornfield, up the hill, turn off towards the next village and then follow the disused railway cutting home. In all, a respectable walk of two miles. The dogs had other ideas. As I led them into the first field, they suddenly realised where they were going and decided to sit down, refusing to go any further. After ten minutes of trying to coax them into the field by throwing sticks and running up and down excitedly, it all failed. So I walked back out of the field, past the dogs, towards home. They both got up and followed me.

My intention of getting fit was not working as planned. I think I need to get new dogs. Perhaps I can trade them for a couple of retired greyhounds. That would sort me out. Not today, though. I've had enough exercise.

※ ※ ※

So, plan B. Eat properly. I read somewhere that we should eat five portions of fruit and vegetables per day. I was planning to cook spit-roast lamb on the barbecue, so I set about calculating. Okay, the oregano sprinkled on the meat is a plant, so that's one. Olive oil comes from an olive, so that's a vegetable. That's number two. The garlic seasoning is also a vegetable, so that's number three. The lamb that is currently going round on the spit only ate grass, so technically that's a vegetable too: number four. The beer that I am holding in my hand is made from hops and malt. That's almost a lentil, so number five. I was planning to put a bit of parsley on the meat before serving, but that's not necessary now.

So although I didn't get much exercise today, I am making up for it by eating properly.

Day 54
TRUST YOURSELVES

16th May 2020

Would you buy a used car from Michael Gove? Most of the population of the UK have realised that he seems shifty and rather sneaky, so the answer is probably no. After all, he was the one that stuffed up Boris Johnson's first attempt at getting the prime minister's job. Boris was well on his way to Number Ten, via the 350-million-pound NHS bus campaign and after confirming that 100 million Turks were arriving next Tuesday. But after promising to throw his weight behind Boris, Gove went to the press and launched his own leadership campaign.

During a BBC interview, he was backed up to the wall and announced that he could categorically guarantee that children are safe to go back to school on the first of June. Then quickly backtracked and stated that the only way to be safe was to stay at home. Still no wiser there, then.

Personally speaking, if Michael Gove told me that it was going to be sunny today, I would get my wellies on, alert the coastguard and be sure to bring a life jacket.

This one statement has now ensured that

even if the schools open as instructed, there will be no children there.

The government's new messages of "Be Alert" and "Use Common Sense" are likely to cause even more confusion. "Stay at Home" worked, and we all did.

First, be alert to what? We can't see the virus because it's really small, so we won't know if it's coming at us. But no problem: if the government wants us to take responsibility rather than them, let's see how that works out.

The Health and Safety Executive will relax regulations on building sites in favour of using common sense. No need to wear a hard hat or high-visibility jacket as it's best not to draw attention to yourselves. Children not attending school because of the closures can again be sent up chimneys. Lumberjacks will no longer be told which side of the branch to sit on while sawing it off. Houses are going to get really big splinters when the cut-down tree falls the wrong way.

Barriers outside shops will be removed to allow stupid people to run into the road to get run over. Traffic lights will be switched off as you should be using common sense if you want to drive. Motorway speed limits will be cancelled as it's okay to go as fast as you feel safe, but stay alert. Best not eat a sandwich and drink a milkshake while driving at 120 mph, though, as this would be silly.

Driving your car home from the pub after nineteen pints of lager and ten whisky chasers would be acceptable provided you felt okay to drive and you were staying alert and using common sense.

My common sense tells me that I should be permitted to visit my mother, sit in her garden two metres apart and have a long-overdue chat. The government don't agree. They consider this to be foolhardy and would rather you come into contact with complete strangers while waiting for hours in a supermarket queue or sitting on a park bench.

My common sense also tells me that you cannot rely on the general population to have any. Some people's idea of common sense is to climb up 5G towers and set fire to them. Jeremy Corbyn's own brother is into that one.

Since Boris returned from his illness long enough to get hammered by Keir Starmer in parliament and went on TV to announce the beginning of the lockdown easing, they generally haven't got a clue what to advise us to do.

So, new government policy is to let us decide, then blame us if things go wrong. We shall see.

Meanwhile, I'm off for a walk to try and get my overweight, unfit dogs in condition, so their overweight, unfit owner can try to reclaim a bit of self-respect.

Day 55
BACK TO WORK

17th May 2020

PETER BARBER

We are still in lockdown and subject to the rules. Most shops still not open, takeaways beginning to wake up but we can't sit down for a meal. Pubs certainly not open yet (I do check every hour). Can't get a haircut, can't go to the dentist to get that filling replaced that I ate last night while chewing on a bag of toffees – I did think it was a hazelnut, though, so not entirely my fault. The only thing that you can go to the shops for is supplies (mostly beer) but no clothes or electrical items or a browse around the bookshop. So we have to resort to window shopping on Amazon apps to arrange our wish list. That will assist the struggling high street. We are all guilty of becoming even more lazy by ordering online. We can sit in our comfy chair, order stuff without going out, and don't even need to carry it home. In the future the high street will be populated by nail salons, hairdressers and betting shops. All retail business will cease to exist as we have now found a better way to go shopping by only using our thumbs.

Boris has sent us back to work while telling us to avoid public transport. Then he switches on the London congestion charge zone cameras so we have pay more than we earn to get there. Nurses and doctors doing the night shift have to pay it twice a day if they are not rich and happen to be living outside the Central London zone, as the hours have increased to catch them too.

Faithful to government advice, I am still going to my office to look out of that window. Bugger all to do, but at least I'm contributing to the recovery by being there. Perhaps the phone will ring later. You never know, I might get lucky.

The problem with my business is that I run a company that requires working in people's homes. They really don't want us there, and who can blame them? They have spent months being told to stay at home, protecting themselves against catching the virus and doing as they were told to protect the NHS, and are hesitant to believe the government advice about letting a team of sweaty workers into their purified homes when they are not even allowed a visit from their mother or sister. So, allowing a team of workers to dig holes in their basements is rather difficult to understand when they can't even sit in the garden and have a cup of coffee with Dad.

The government really doesn't want you to think too much about it, though, and continues to throw slogans at you so at least it will look like they have the right idea. It worked for Brexit – why not now?

So today I am going to use my new-found freedom. I will wait until the clock ticks around to 4 p.m. Get in my car. Leave my permitted workplace, pass by the permitted garden centre to buy a plant (don't really need one, but do want to use the opportunity). Will pass by the pub to check if it's open yet. If not, off to the supermarket for a couple of cases of beer as I am allowed to buy it without getting other essentials. Go home, take the dogs for a walk, then go out for another one. Come home and relax, knowing that I have today done everything permitted. It was a bit like I did yesterday, but who's keeping score?

If the gymnasium was open, I would have gone for a workout. I hear that they have a new jacuzzi. But maybe I'll just sit in the garden and have a beer. After all, it's been a long day.

Day 56

FREEDOM AT LAST

18th May 2020

Now we seem to be leaving the lockdown. Traffic is starting to get back to normal. Local councils have woken up their road repair crews and started to ship out temporary traffic lights to ensure that when the traffic starts moving properly again, they can make sure that it does not.

Queues of cars are starting to block roads around McDonald's and Kentucky Fried Chicken drive-throughs, with people suffering withdrawal symptoms after missing their favourite fast food for the last two months. Discarded Big Mac boxes and empty milkshake containers are beginning to build up on grass verges, and the urban wildlife is now back to its diet of thrown-away KFC bones.

Things that make us laugh have changed. When I was a kid, we used to laugh at people walking around dressed as chickens. People slipping on banana skins were a long-term source of amusement. During this lockdown our humour has become more sophisticated. Long gone are the racist jokes of old. Punchlines seem to be a thing of the past and have been replaced by cartoons and illustrations on social media showing a different view on life related to our own experiences. We are now laughing at ourselves and sharing it. Comedy now comes from looking at normal life or news events and seeing the funny side. It's all about perception. I would never have imagined that I would be amused by walking around a supermarket or counting the number of items in other shoppers' baskets from behind a bit of tape on the floor while standing two metres away.

Making my daughter laugh with my persistence trying to adopt the family guinea pigs as I have got bored with the normal barbecue ingredients. Her having hours of fun trying to catch a squirrel in the vain attempt to pass it off to me and save her family pets (I haven't given up on that one yet).

Laughing at myself with my fear of running out of beer, and trying to drink myself to death and finding it funny. Probably not actually funny, but it does seem like it after four beers.

Anyway, it's been fun. But this will be my last daily post for a while. I really do need to stop doing nothing and go back to work to earn a living before I starve, but more importantly run out of beer.

I have been writing these texts for the last 56 days without a break, and I would never have imagined that I could keep this going for so long. But there is so much out there that makes me laugh. Trump has been particularly useful as he is always good for amusement. Boris seems to be out of his depth, but I am still angry with him over Brexit, so he will never be trusted.

History will judge this world crisis in the future and see how the British government handled it. As we are likely to be the worst affected country in Europe, and perhaps even the world, it is unlikely to be a favourable legacy.

For my next project I may look at compiling a new barbecue cookbook. This will include traditional recipes together with other exotic dishes, starting with guinea pigs. No bats, though. I promise.

Thanks to all my pals who have taken the time to read this stuff. I hope it made you smile at least once a day. I know that I laughed every day writing it.

Love, Peter

About the Author

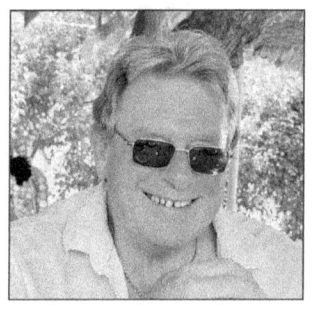

Peter Barber was born in Watford, in the UK, and flits between Bedfordshire and Athens with his Greek wife. He spends as much time as possible in Greece messing about in boats, enjoying the weather and the company, but mostly the food and wine.

THE PARTHENON SERIES:

Book 1: *A Parthenon on our Roof*
Book 2: *A Parthenon in Pefki*
Book 3: *The Parthenon Paradox*

PETER BARBER'S MUSINGS

Book 1: *Musings from a Greek Village*
Book 2: *Musings from a Pandemic*

CREDITS

I wish to give a big thanks to my editor, Nicky Talyor. She guided me through the rewrite and prevented most of my incoherent ramblings.

Thank you to Ant Press, especially Victoria Twead, whose patience and persistence ensured this book was the best it could be.

Contacts and Links

Email: peterbarberbooks@gmail.com
Website: https://peterbarberwriter.com/
Facebook: www.facebook.com/peter.barber.771/
Twitter: www.twitter.com/greekwriting

Writing About Greece

Join the Facebook community, Writing about Greece, a group founded by Peter Barber and his wife, Alex, dedicated to Greece and people who love Greece.

www.facebook.com/groups/369010324939088
or type
Writing About Greece in the Facebook search box.

We Love Memoirs

Join Peter Barber and other memoir authors and readers in the **We Love Memoirs Facebook group**, the friendliest group on Facebook.

www.facebook.com/groups/welovememoirs/

More Ant Press Books

AWESOME AUTHORS ~ AWESOME BOOKS

If you enjoyed this book, you may also enjoy these other Ant Press memoir series. All titles are available in ebook, paperback, hardback and large print editions from **Amazon**.

These two booksellers offer FREE delivery worldwide.
Blackwells.co.uk and **Wordery.com**

More Stores
Waterstones (Europe delivery), **Booktopia** (Australia), **Barnes & Noble** (USA), and all good bookstores.

PETER BARBER
Award-winning bestselling author

The Parthenon Series

1. A Parthenon on our Roof

2. A Parthenon in Pefki
3. The Parthenon Paradox

Peter Barber's Musings

1. Musings from a Greek Village
2. Musings from a Pandemic

VICTORIA TWEAD
New York Times bestselling author

The Old Fools Series

1. Chickens, Mules and Two Old Fools
2. Two Old Fools ~ Olé!
3. Two Old Fools on a Camel
4. Two Old Fools in Spain Again
5. Two Old Fools in Turmoil
6. Two Old Fools Down Under
7. Two Old Fools Fair Dinkum

One Young Fool in Dorset (Prequel)
One Young Fool in South Africa (Prequel)

Dear Fran, Love Dulcie: Life and Death in the Hills and Hollows of Bygone Australia

BETH HASLAM

The Fat Dogs series

Fat Dogs and French Estates ~ Part I
Fat Dogs and French Estates ~ Part II
Fat Dogs and French Estates ~ Part III
Fat Dogs and French Estates ~ Part IV
Fat Dogs and French Estates ~ Part V
Fat Dogs and Welsh Estates ~ The Prequel

DIANE ELLIOTT

Lady Goatherder series

Butting Heads in Spain: Lady Goatherder 1
El Maestro: Lady Goatherder 2

EJ BAUER

The Someday Travels series

From Moulin Rouge to Gaudi's City

From Gaudi's City to Granada's Red Palace
From an Umbrian Farmhouse to Como's Quiet Shores

NICK ALBERT

Fresh Eggs and Dog Beds series

Fresh Eggs and Dog Beds: Living the Dream in Rural Ireland
Fresh Eggs and Dog Beds 2: Still Living the Dream in Rural Ireland
Fresh Eggs and Dog Beds 3: More Living the Dream in Rural Ireland
Fresh Eggs and Dog Beds 4: More Living the Dream in Rural Ireland

For more information about stockists, Ant Press titles or how to publish with Ant Press, please visit our website or contact us by email.

WEBSITE: www.antpress.org

EMAIL: admin@antpress.org

FACEBOOK: https://www.facebook.com/AntPress/

INSTAGRAM: https://instagram.com/publishwithantpress

www.ingramcontent.com/pod-product-compliance
Lightning Source LLC
Chambersburg PA
CBHW072048110526
44590CB00018B/3084